What People Are Saying

Be Diffe.

Be Different is Marty Strong's third treatise on leadership. This work completes his high impact trinity of successful books on leadership, strategy, and innovation. When I read Marty's first book, *Be Nimble*, I found myself not only nodding my head in agreement with his concepts but was eager to immediately put his wisdom into motion within my company. I got to know Marty personally over time; he even appeared several times as a guest on my *Elevate Your Leadership* podcast. I've benefitted as a CEO from his generous mentorship and insightful business wisdom. In early 2023, it was with high expectations that I ordered *Be Visionary*, Marty's second book. When I began to read this second book on vision and strategy, I was once again energized by Marty's straightforward, conversational, and often funny narratives, relating what he learned after 20 years in the SEAL Teams, and twenty-plus years leading commercial businesses. *Be Different* reminds me of the creativity and innovation I witnessed in my 26 years as a Navy Special Operations Bomb Technician, a profession where we always had to get it right. Challenging the status quo is a necessary part of evolution in business and in life. *Be Different* provides the reader with the methods and tools to defuse their "business bombs" and advance their creative initiatives in an unconventional and innovative manner.

Robert Pizzini
US Navy Special Operations Veteran, CEO, and
Best-Selling Author of *Elevate Your Leadership*

Marty Strong leads, trains, and engages like a commander focused on the horizon, the objective, and the welfare of his people. When I read *Be Nimble*, followed by *Be Visionary*, I thought I was back in the military training senior commanders how to think not only tactically but strategically. To exercise judgment, and to lead. Marty writes in such a way that you see his experience unfold right in front of you, here and now, communicated in such a careful narrative manner you can easily absorb his insights and make them your own. Marty's skills, passion, and empathy for others are a gift. I read his works and understand why those who were trained by him and served with him in the military and in corporate business have remained close to him ever since, friends for life. I encourage and invite everyone to join the ranks and become inspired by reading Marty's door-opening books.

Michael Steiner
Executive Director .
BEST Robotics, Inc.

Be Different is not written from a point of recklessness and disregard for habits, incrementalism, and rules—quite the opposite. This book is constantly treading between following, bending, ignoring, and making new rules, between baby steps and wild leaps. And the five steps to change ourselves into thinking differently attest to Marty's focus on balance: a self-inventory on what is blocking us; self-discipline; self-awareness; self-esteem; and self-lessness. If you think you are too unconventional or insufficiently creative, *Be Different* will still give you practical help in leading an innovative self, teams, and organizations.

Marco Dondi
Successful Author and Expert Associate Partner, McKinsey & Company, Geneva, Switzerland

Be Different

How Navy SEALs and Entrepreneurs
Bend, Break, or Ignore the Rules to
Get Results!

Be Different

How Navy SEALs and Entrepreneurs Bend, Break, or Ignore the Rules to Get Results!

Marty Strong

CEO and Chief Strategy Officer
Retired SEAL Officer and Combat Veteran
BBA, MA, Lean Six Sigma Blackbelt

BUSINESS
BOOKS

London, UK
Washington, DC, USA

CollectiveInk

First published by Business Books, 2024
Business Books is an imprint of Collective Ink Ltd.,
Unit 11, Shepperton House, 89 Shepperton Road, London, N1 3DF
office@collectiveink.com
www.collectiveinkbooks.com
www.collectiveinkbooks.com/business-books/

For distributor details and how to order please visit the 'Ordering' section on our website.

Text copyright: Marty Strong 2023

ISBN: 978 1 80341 133 0
978 1 80341 703 5 (ebook)
Library of Congress Control Number: 2023948913

A CIP catalogue record for this book is available from the British Library.

Design: Lapiz Digital Services

UK: Printed and bound by CPI Group (UK) Ltd, Croydon, CR0 4YY
Printed in North America by CPI GPS partners

Contents

Other Titles by This Author

*Be Nimble: How the Creative Navy SEAL Mindset Wins
on the Battlefield and in Business*
ISBN 978-1789048407

Be Visionary: Strategic Leadership in the Age of Optimization
ISBN 978-1785354328

Time Warrior Sagas

A Time for Glory: The Time Warrior Sagas Book One
ISBN 978-0999481035

A Time for Honor: The Time Warrior Sagas Book Two
ISBN 978-0999481059

A Time for Truth: The Time Warrior Sagas Book Three
ISBN 978-0999481028

A Time for Rebellion: The Time Warrior Sagas Book Four
ISBN 978-0999481066

Seal Strike Series

Death Before Dawn: Seal Strike Book 1
ISBN 978-0999481097

The Warrior Code: Seal Strike Book 2
ISBN 978-0999481080

The Brotherhood: Seal Strike Book 3
ISBN 978-0999481073

In the Shadow of Evil: Seal Strike Book 4
ISBN 978-1735050195

Kandahar Moon: Seal Strike Book 5
ISBN 978-1735050188

Preface

Disruption Is the Law of the Universe

In the late 1980s, the catchall label assigned to describe elite units across all the military services was changed from Unconventional Warfare to Special Operations. The newly formed US Special Operations Command took a step further, creating five separate and unique special operations performance areas. At the time it seemed logical, but after years of experience in institutional design and human performance, I realize this organizational effort was a mistake. It was a corporate move, a move to become more efficient, to establish tighter control; and while well-intentioned, it was probably a miscalculation. Being unconventional was a *mindset*, not a mission category. It was the core operating system that made these famous elite units effective, agile, and feared. It was this mindset that set us apart. We were different, but in a good way, a Jedi knight sort of way. We were tasked with doing weird things; out-of-the-box things; the things conventional units, and more to the point, conventional thinking, couldn't solve. Being organized is critical to the health and welfare of any organization, but understanding the role divergent thinking, creativity, and freedom of design play in an organization's success is also essential.

Be Different: How Navy SEALs and Entrepreneurs Bend, Break, or Ignore the Rules to Get Results! is all about unconventional thinking. This book focuses on the application of thinking differently, acting differently, and applying this refreshing and enlightening methodology to succeed, to win, whatever winning means for you or your organization. Come with me on this quest to discover just how easy it is to be creative, to be innovative, to make a difference, to change the world!

Be different, stay different!

Marty Strong

Foreword

In my almost 15 years at McKinsey, now leading McKinsey's research and several programs related to skills, I am fully convinced that what a person knows or how capable a person is have diminishing importance compared to how they think and behave. Once existing Artificial Intelligence is adopted at scale, most of the work left will be non-routine. Addressing climate change will require unleashing a giant wave of innovation and rapid adoption of new technologies. In *Be Different*, Marty helps us develop one of the most important mindsets in this age where we are in dire need of innovation: unconventional thinking.

What brought an unconventional McKinsey consultant authoring *Outgrowing Capitalism* to cross paths with a Navy SEAL turned serial entrepreneur and author? We met in the boardroom of BEST Robotics, Inc., a volunteer-based organization that develops creativity in tens of thousands of kids every year, and under Marty's leadership is now trying to develop creativity in adults as well. But Marty's bond with creativity is rooted much earlier from his time commanding Navy SEAL missions and developing the unconventional mindset in himself, in others, and more importantly, codifying the recipe for us into this book.

I have been fascinated by Marty's stories and how he translates the learning from these extreme situations into simple but non-obvious tips that can help us, and our organizations, unleash innovative mindsets and practices. What is obvious is the root cause of the problem, which Marty captures very well: "it's a significant emotional breakthrough to admit there is a problem; and that addiction is adherence to silly rules, outdated procedures, defunct processes, flawed systems, and worn-out traditions."

Among my favorite parts of *Be Different* is the process to overcome this problem and unlock unconventional thinking. The first step is intellectual humility: I was once given the feedback of suffering from "expert-itis" and this first step therefore particularly resonates with me. Without humility we can't let in insights that are far from what we already know. The second step: intellectual curiosity. If humility allows the open mind, then curiosity can lead to the exploration of new ideas, the ability to go much further than "been there, done that." Only as a third step comes intellectual creativity, which although easier at a young age, Marty explains throughout the book how to unlock it again at any age.

But along the journey to unlock non-incremental innovation in people and organization, Marty dispenses deep reflections and suggestions that will stay with you. He brings an interesting parallel between tight-knit communities and how colleagues should behave with each other. Colleagues spend much of their time with each other but for some reason do not display the same level of care and genuine intention to help each other that tight-knit communities do. Consequently, we often lack a safe space for the crazy ideas to be voiced and for non-incremental change to be embraced.

His military stories lead into another of his most valuable analogies: to think about transformations, innovations, change initiatives and new ventures as if they were a mission. You start with creativity and unconventional thinking but then proceed with precise planning and readiness to improvise as things play out differently than can be anticipated.

Be Different is not written from a point of recklessness and disregard for habits, incrementalism, and rules—quite the opposite. This book is constantly treading between following, bending, ignoring, and making new rules, between baby steps and wild leaps. And the five steps to change ourselves into thinking differently attest to Marty's focus on balance:

a self-inventory on what is blocking us; self-discipline; self-awareness; self-esteem; and self-lessness. If you think you are too unconventional or insufficiently creative, *Be Different* will still give you practical help in leading an innovative self, teams, and organizations.

Marco Dondi
Successful Author and Expert Associate Partner, McKinsey & Company, Geneva, Switzerland

Acknowledgments

When I sat down to write *Be Nimble* in late 2019, I never dreamed my quest to understand the complexities of dynamic leadership would lead to writing three books. However, here I am and here we are, taking yet one more leap of faith that I can deliver a wholesome and enticing thesis on how being different is wonderful and worth pursuing. As I note throughout *Be Different*, I began learning about divergent thinking and the evolving brain science related to human creativity when I joined the board of BEST Robotics, Inc. in the winter of 2022. It was an experience that transformed my purely practical and entrepreneurial understanding of innovation to one of scientific enlightenment. This book was a labor of love for me, and without many notable mentors and advisors I would have never completed the work. Chief among these incredible thought leaders is Michael Steiner, Executive Director of BEST Robotics, Inc. It was Michael who charmed me into joining his crusade to help underserved youth to discover their inner potential and to love creativity. I also want to thank my brain trust, two people who have guided my mind and my pen through all three books in this series, Chuck Rushworth and Lee Priest. Finally, I want to thank my wife Michele for allowing me to carve out from our lives the time it takes to conceive, design, develop, and complete a book like *Be Different*!

Chapter One

Introduction

The mind, once stretched by a new idea, never returns to its original dimensions.
Ralph Waldo Emerson

My father was a self-taught artist, painter, and musician. As a depression-era farm boy, he started sketching the barns, animals, and landscape around him using a piece of coal. After my grandfather was killed in a tragic tractor accident, my grandmother sold the farm and moved her five children into the city. There, my father continued to follow his muse, sketching factories, cityscapes, and any old jumble of industrial still life.

For a canvas, he used old, roll-down window shades poached from abandoned buildings. The shades were made of a stiff material called Holland linen. He'd straighten them, using strips of wood as a frame, making it easier for his charcoal lump to glide across the smooth light-yellow surface. Somewhere in his early teens, he took up the harmonica. That led to accordions, pianos, and guitars. He never learned to read music; yet he was masterful with each instrument.

My father wasn't a touchy feely sort of man. He was quiet to the extreme. Self-absorbed in his work, his art, and his music. In a time when children were required to ask permission before speaking, it made for a strange relationship. When I was in second grade, there was a school talent show. I came home excited to participate, but keenly aware I had no talent to show. While listening to my mother rattle off options, my father walked into the kitchen and said, "You'll play the guitar and sing a song."

I looked at my stone-faced father, dumbfounded and confused on several levels. I didn't know how to play anything, and I couldn't sing. What's more, my father never involved himself in my life in a positive way. My mother's face was also in a state of shock, and I just sat there like a lump. Over the next six weeks my father taught me to play one song on his acoustic guitar. "Beautiful Brown Eyes." He wrote down the words, too, told me to memorize them and practice singing while playing.

My father was a country music fan and thought it would be easier to play the guitar using a bar. This was a solid steel device approximately three inches long and an inch wide. It was flat on one side; this side was placed on the strings. You slid the bar up and down the neck of the guitar to change the chords; it worked. I was able to play the music and sing the song. I was ready on game day.

All I remember from that day was failure and embarrassment. I walked onto the stage and sat down on a chair placed at the edge of the stage. I looked up at the crowd of over 50 parents and kids, and took a deep breath and began to channel my inner Elvis. About a quarter way through the song, my hands sweaty from anxiety, the bar squirted from my hand, bounced once, and disappeared into a rectangular slot on the edge of the stage. Gone. I froze. Without the bar, I couldn't finish. I started to freak out, then to cry. A teacher walked over and guided me off the stage. I've never learned to play an instrument to this day.

Art was another experience all together. From an early age I remember sitting quietly watching my father sketch his concepts on white canvas. No more charcoal—he had a full painter's kit, multiple easels, palette boards, brushes, and oil paint arrayed like colorful soldiers, ready to play their part. For some reason it all made perfect sense to me. The process, the preparation, the attention to concept first, then the minute details. I think my father understood this, because after a while he began to teach me. First the concepts of light, shape, color, and texture. He was an avid user of palette knives, creating a three-dimensional aspect to his work.

The next phase in my development was learning how to sketch. My father explained how to use shapes like circles, ovals, squares, and rectangles, to create the conceptual outlines of almost anything. Using this trick, I could draw still lifes, faces, and eventually anything that I fancied. This period of interaction and learning was cut short when he accepted a job with the US Army in Saigon, Vietnam. He was gone for almost four years; but I had the bug bad, so I continued to draw and develop as an artist without his tutelage.

My father's interaction with me in those first ten years of my life were less training, coaching, and mentoring than it was a silent parental challenge to try and not quit. My father never shared his opinion of me as a kid, and in fact only told me he was proud of me twice before he passed at the age of 76. The first time was in a bar in Detroit. I was home from Army parachute school at Fort Benning, Georgia, after graduating the Navy's BUD/S, or basic SEAL training course. After I explained that I was a Navy frogman, he smiled and nodded, took a sip of his Old Grandad and soda, then said, "That's impressive. We carried those guys on my destroyer during Korea."

The second time my father provided a positive critique was after he'd binge read my first novel. He was a big-time lover of books and reading in general, so I think in his eyes I'd moved from his kid to a whole new level of adult. He left us soon after telling me how much he loved the book, and never got to read the next ten I wrote. I like to think he would have approved of them all.

I don't remember when I decided to become a writer, but I can remember that by the time I was 11 I was receiving praise for my imaginative storytelling. As with most things, praise meant positive attention, so I started writing more and more. At this stage in my life, I was drawing Marvel comic book heroes in minute and accurate detail and writing a journal. Every writing assignment in school was a chance to shine, and I poured my heart into the task. By the time I joined the Navy at 17, I was sure those days were behind me. I was wrong.

Writing on the Job

Military writing is not filled with flowery prose, exotic words, or passionate themes. It is stilted and bland. Military writing falls into several categories of boring. There are plans, lists, orders, and reports. The language is screened, scrubbed, reviewed, and agonized over by the entire chain of command. By the time I was 19 and working as an enlisted frogman assigned to SEAL Team Two, I'd demonstrated several skills useful to SEAL officers.

In those days, briefings were presented on four-foot-by-three-foot pads of paper hung from an easel. If you could draw a straight line and had nice calligraphy, you were hired to transfer the plans from a yellow legal pad to the larger display. If you could draw or recreate maps and terrain features, you would have a special power unrelated to the commando job. Once I was found out, I never escaped this task in one way or another for the rest of my Navy career.

The positive side effect of drawing and transcribing mission language was I spent a lot of time watching and listening to the SEAL mission planners do their thing. Most of them were multi-tour Vietnam combat veterans and smart. As time went on, I became adept at seeing things. I occasionally began to toss out an insight here or an idea there. For a few years my comments would elicit an amused smile or a stern glance. Eventually my thoughts began to be received differently. I was still a junior enlisted SEAL, but I had a knack for conceptualizing missions; and the more I learned, the more my inputs were accepted at face value.

I'm telling you this because one form of creativity blended and merged into another form of creative thinking until the three (drawing, writing, and planning) became as easy as walking down the street for me. It was around this time, after six years in the SEAL Teams, that senior leaders began talking to me about becoming an officer. I didn't have a degree yet, a prerequisite in the Navy before becoming an officer. I spent the next two years finishing two years of courses and then transferred from SEAL Team Two in Virginia Beach, Virginia, to Coronado, California, to instruct the basis SEAL course.

Officer Bound

I finished my degree two years after arriving in California and was selected for officer candidate school in Newport, Rhode Island. At BUD/s and in my studies in college, the writing was as stilted as ever. My business degree didn't require poetry or character development. Neither did the curriculum I wrote while an instructor at BUD/S. After graduating from officer candidate school, I was ordered to SEAL Team Four in Virginia Beach. I was a known entity on the East Coast, and soon I was sucked into high-level contingency planning and eventually briefing the plans to generals and admirals. Not much different from my days at SEAL Team Two.

I began to hit my stride, and became a creative planner and thinker. I've shared my experiences on significant military projects and will share more with you in this book. It was heady stuff. I was punching several levels above my rank; but the funny thing was, I was doing so due to a lack of inspired competition. It wasn't anyone's fault; it was that they were products of their conditioning growing up and, more specifically, in the Navy. Risk aversion related to career strategies muted many officers who were senior to me. So did a lack of conceptual creativity in general. They were thinking in two dimensions while I was thinking and planning in three or more.

Now, to be fair I wasn't the only officer like me, but the numbers were small. A lack of training in planning, real planning, mission impossible type planning, was a culprit, too. Little to no mentoring in how to conceive a problem set and work out all the angles was another contributing factor. Since those days, this shortfall has been addressed, and SEAL leaders and senior enlisted advisors are taught how to think and plan divergently. As I came to the end of my 20 years in the Navy, I took with me all the lessons learned from my experiences in creative planning and leadership.

Creativity in the Commercial World

When I took off my uniform for the last time, I assumed I had something to offer as I entered the commercial marketplace. I had a degree in business and a graduate degree in management, was a seasoned leader and knew how to handle stress. As a 20-year military veteran, I assumed creative thinking was an everyday activity in the commercial world. I was wrong. I was also wrong about my value, at least initially.

I began my new career a bit fearful and humbled by what I didn't know. I realized I needed to become an apprentice, and look, listen, and learn. I'd gone from the top of one game to the bottom of another, and it wasn't pleasant. Creativity wasn't the name of the game, flexibility and adaptability was. My willingness to fight through this period of my life and not quit, to force myself to become a student and learn, and my capacity for stress management were the differentiators that allowed me to survive. After two years, only six of my original class of 41 financial advisors were still in the business. In the end I was different because I survived, not because I was better.

After eight years managing money, I realized that old conceptual thinking skills were alive and well in me. I was a good money manager, and even better than average when the markets and the economy became turbulent. My clients appreciated my poise and my long-term view. Near the end of this career, I was pulled back into an old role. During the Global War on Terror, I shifted away from the financial industry and became first a counter-terrorism consultant and then an executive at a defense contracting firm. It was this last career move that finally allowed me to leverage all my experience, education, failures, and successes.

Becoming an Entrepreneur

For the last 15 years, I've been a student in a different sort of school. Building and leading departments, divisions, and companies is exhilarating and terrifying. Both rewarding and debilitating. I learned to be open to all information and to never ever rest on my laurels. I eventually found myself studying extremely sharp business leaders, and at the same time responsible for coaching and mentoring my leadership team. This teacher-student workstyle made sense at the time, and it still does. Being different isn't about being the best at the expense of others' well-being and professional progress. Being different is so much more!

For most of you I suggest taking this path. Teaching is its own reward; and if you lift up your leaders, they in turn will lift up their teams. Practice intellectual and professional humility by playing the student. Learn everything you can about things you don't know. Seek mentors and champions to emulate and listen to. Being different is a continuum of lifelong risk taking and discovery. It never ends, and that's why being different is so much fun!

Becoming a Speaker and Author

I always loved reading, and as a young boy began to experiment with writing, too. It was in middle school that I realized writing was not only fun, but also a way to get my thoughts onto a piece of paper. If you love to read books, then you have a deep appreciation and respect for authors. My dad taught me that words reflected thoughts and ideas and, once captured, could last for thousands of years. To me, books represented a time capsule; and if I could write one, I would live on forever.

Of course, juvenile dreams are fleeting. I soon wanted to be a lead guitar player in a rock band but that never happened. Writing in high school was less challenging, but just barely. My teachers issued assignments that were aimed at the median skill level in the class. I didn't have a problem with passing, but I did decide to exceed the requirements on a regular basis. My writing style was logical and tight. My teachers were happy, and therefore I received a lot of positive reinforcement.

In my last two years of school, I took almost exclusively college preparatory courses. My critical thinking and writing skills were sufficient to get a B if I wanted to slack off. I didn't. Instead, I took the challenge head-on and worked harder to write better. At this point, my teachers were telling me I had the makings of lawyer and that my parents should consider sending me to law school after college. I wasn't sure what a lawyer did, but the praise was flattering, nonetheless. What the teachers didn't know was that despite my 4.0 grade point average throughout high school, my dad had already told me he wasn't paying for college. End of discussion.

Fast forward to my later Naval career, working on thought projects and seeking inspiration about the future of the SEAL Teams. I watched and learned from seasoned thinkers and writers. Professionals who knew how to influence people and events through their skill with words. I noticed there were few who were both adept at writing and public speaking. I became a student and strived to achieve success in both categories.

When I decided to write my first novel some 20 years later, it felt daunting. Despite my experience with the written word, becoming a novelist was not intuitive or easy. I was too structured, a hangover from technical writing for over 30 years. I didn't know how to develop a story arc or compelling characters. I didn't know how to make dialogue between characters sound natural. Heck, I didn't know how to write dialogue at all. I wanted it so bad that I started reading everything I could find on the subject. In time, I began to experiment and learn. It came slow, painfully slow.

The epiphany hit me one day while I was trying to write a chapter of my first novel, a science fiction story focused on time travel. I was writing, editing, writing, and editing. Frustrated, I decided to take a break for a week or so. When I came back to the project, I decided to ignore the editing and just write, and that's when the magic happened. I couldn't stop. I found out later this was called stream of consciousness writing. Letting the story and the characters flow naturally without edits or inspection. And that was that. I became a writer.

Nine novels and two business books later (*Be Different* is number three), it's hard to believe I struggled so mightily in the beginning, but I did. Having faith, being open-minded, and letting the creative juices take control was the solution. As you'll see in this book, I believe it's the solution for a lot of creative endeavors.

Creativity Is a Journey

This is a book about applied creativity. How dreaming, visualizing, conceptualizing, and converting these musings into a new method, a new path, can change the world and your life. It is my opinion that institutions of all types have done us a disservice by conditioning us to think and act the same. Not for nefarious reasons, just because it's easier to make us all dance to the same intellectual tune—less discord, less confusion. So we grow up and grow old, accepting things the way they are, based predominantly on the past. This is why change is so hard for most of us. Change feels like rebellion.

I believe in physical barriers and controls, through lawful means, for the purpose of public health, safety, and restraining crime. In fact, I feel most rules, regulations, and compliance are well intended. However, I strongly feel our history of continuous external conditioning—teaching and cajoling us how to think, what to think—is a significant reason we all struggle to use our minds the way they are designed to be used. It is a reason we shy away from change and see alteration as a threat.

Learning to strip away this conditioning, to become honest and open-minded, is a positive behavior that will set you on a journey of creativity and innovative discovery. I will explore this with you and provide examples that illustrate how conditioning inhibits understanding and imagination, and what happens when we learn to embrace the wonder and inspiring power of the human mind.

We will transition from understanding what we are up against to grasping how we can leverage inspiration and imagination in life and in our work. The world is an incredibly diverse and fantastic place. However, we spend most of our lives ignorant of much of this due to distance, boundaries, personal resources, and, yes, conditioning in the form of culture, traditions, and fear of what is different. It's time to embrace different, to feel different, to be different.

My journey from failed musician at the talent show to published author and CEO is but one of millions of similar journeys that others have taken to learn about themselves, their environment, and the power of their minds. My hope is that you patiently read through my thesis and step away more aware and more motivated to reignite your personal creativity. I'm convinced inspiration and imagination can make our planet a more interesting and enlightened place for all of us. Enjoy!

Chapter Two

Stability Is an Illusion

Stability can only be attained by inactive matter.
Marie Curie

I grew up watching old World War Two movies with my dad. Most were black and white and most followed a similar patriotic story arc. By the late 1950s and early 1960s, a new variation in the tried-and-true hero-wins-every-time story appeared. This twist involved misfits, even criminals. This new story arc went like this—a conventional force, led by conventional leaders, was faced with an unconventional challenge. The challenge encountered also was strategically or operationally critical to victory, however victory was defined.

To the alarm and dismay of many officers and senior enlisted leaders, a special unit was created to handle the challenge. A suicide squad for a suicide mission. Expendable to be sure, even more so because the special unit was going to be led by and filled with—you guessed it—losers. Sounds counterintuitive, right? Wouldn't you send your best and brightest? Well maybe not, especially if your best and brightest were traditionalists, conformists, and individuals, incapable of nonlinear thinking. That's where being an enigma comes in handy.

The Devil's Brigade, The Dirty Dozen, Kelly's Heroes, and many more of these deviant-themed war movies were produced and, surprisingly, were highly successful. The idea was simple. Unconventional thinkers, dreamers, geniuses, creatives, and people with overactive imaginations were pariahs in the strict control structure of the US military in the early part of the twentieth century. No wonder they were always in trouble or, worse, in jail. And no wonder their characters were able to come up with insane plans that succeeded in crushing the unconventional challenge. It wasn't until the 1980s before special operations units were truly allowed to thrive and become a permanent part of the US military. Before that, they were disposed of as fast as they were created.

The Case for Instability

When I was 11 years old, my family moved to Japan. At the time I was quite happy living a simple American life in Omaha, Nebraska. It was where all my friends lived. My grandma, uncles, aunts, and cousins were only an hour away in Sioux City, Iowa. Life was good. Moving to Japan was a shock, especially for my mom; she never recovered. Four years later, my parents were divorced and my sister, brother, and I were back in Omaha. Life would take another turn for the worse, as before long, my mom sank into depression, alcoholism, and mental illness.

I learned at age 11 that stability and normality were fragile concepts. When I moved to Japan, it took me six months to fit in, to gain new friendships. It was the same when I returned to America. After valiantly trying to play the surrogate "man of the house," I fled to live with my dad who had moved to Oahu, Hawaii. It was the same thing all over again. Seeking new friends, getting over the loss of my old friends, trying to fit in and trying to achieve stability. It was after two years and another move, this time to Grosse Pointe, Michigan, that I decided stability and normalcy were not in the cards. I also decided to stop assimilating and carve out my own brand, my own sense of destiny.

Throughout the ages, being different and—more importantly—thinking differently have stirred both positive and negative emotions. Societies and their functional subsets, governments, tribes, clans, family, and guilds—to name a few—held conformity in high regard. Nonconformity was ridiculed, ignored, or worse, stamped out as a threat to stability. Thankfully, today we live in a more enlightened world that often rewards divergent thought and applauds breakthrough creativity. However, while we no longer live in medieval times, there is still an institutionalized reliance on conformity of action and thought. Stasis is comfortable, change is not.

When I was young, I found out quickly that my energy and insight weren't appreciated; more, they wasn't tolerated. Without experience and positional authority, I wasn't credible. Without ingesting and memorizing very specific knowledge from only approved sources, my ideas and insights were considered irrelevant. I was told things like stay in my lane, stick to my limited entry level role, or leave the thinking and problem solving to upper management. Being told how to think and — worse — not to think was frustrating for me, and I soon learned it was burdensome and debilitating for many other people, too.

The Stability Imperative

Being different and thinking differently isn't hard to do, but it's oftentimes challenging in the face of social and organizational pressure to conform. Innovative thinking that intends to incite change is perceived by many as destructive — that's right, a threat. The question is: why? Why is creativity perceived by so many people as a danger to be mitigated? I believe the answer lies in the way societies, large and small, strive to control their populations through obedience, compliance, and risk intolerance.

Companies follow a similar governance approach. It is interesting to note here that if you ask people if they like their vehicles, their smart phones, their Bluetooth-enabled devices, the response would be yes! Yet each of these expressions of creative genius displaced something else. They altered, shifted, or destroyed the status quo, and by doing so became prophecy fulfilled. Change is disruptive, and there is a price to pay for progress.

Technology has consistently improved human quality of life for the last ten thousand years. Ironically, once new technology has been adopted, humans find they never want to go back to the days when it didn't exist. Of course, this loving embrace only occurs after a healthy phase of rejection, mockery, and denial, before grudgingly adopting and embracing the new normal. Most other forms of innovative change unrelated to technology go through this same cycle of slow acceptance.

Technology is easy to see, feel, use, and perhaps appreciate. Other forms of creative change, such as organizational redesign, bold business strategies, or conversion to hybrid work processes are not so easy to understand. This inherent subtlety makes it more challenging to explain the benefits in a way most can grasp and accept. It defies easy communication, and trust me when I say that effective communication is the key to effective change management and acceptance.

A few years ago, I toured a local office space before conducting a business development call with a potential client. The vice president leading me around the space was proud of their innovative approach to workplace dynamics. There was an open-concept floor plan. Multiple meeting rooms available to all on a first-come, first-served basis. Everywhere else was filled with desks. Each desk had a low, twelve-inch carpeted privacy barrier. Just enough to hide the person in front of and beside you, but low enough to stand up and have a conversation. I loved it! By the time the meeting was over, I knew what I had to do.

The next day I met with my CFO and COO to discuss my brainchild. We were going to open the office space and create an environment more conducive to communication, eye contact, empathy, and morale. My CFO was instantly against the idea. Accountants need privacy, and the existing eight-foot-high cubicle walls provided that privacy. My COO listened to the CFO and nodded his head. He agreed with the privacy part, but then said he'd hated the egg carton feel of the office for a long time. Maybe there was a compromise that would work?

I bit my tongue and waited until they'd both had their say. Many of the accountants wore headsets and ear buds already to gain privacy while crunching numbers. Could we buy the employees sound-suppressing headsets, and then move forward with my big idea? Over the next few days, I thought about this concept; and the more I did, the more I resolved myself to make it happen. There was one more element I began to consider, a change that would directly attack the perceived perks and pecking order of my headquarters' employees.

When I appeared in the plush offices of Legg Mason Wood Walker in downtown Baltimore, Maryland, I was stepping into a world as unlike a SEAL Team as you can imagine. The entire 18-story building was sheathed in green windows, making it look like a magical place. Everyone was courteous; and as I proceeded through an aptitude test and six separate vetting interviews, I couldn't help but notice how proper and corporate everything appeared. That is until I was directed to my final interview.

I arrived on the top floor of the emerald tower and sought out the COO's secretary. She was pleasant and asked me to wait. I looked around and noticed everyone was working diligently. A hand on my shoulder made me spin around, and the secretary smiled. "Normally the COO is at his desk," she said, pointing, "but he would like to meet you up in the executive lounge instead." I looked where she pointed and noted the simple office desk sitting in the open near the center of the room.

I scanned the perimeter of the senior executive floor and saw it was ringed with opulent offices, glass half walls allowing the sunlight to flow through into the main space where we stood. Each office was appointed with high-end furniture, and art adorned the two walls that were not made of glass. I then looked back at the secretary and asked her why the number two person at Legg Mason didn't have an office. She smiled and began to guide me toward the elevator. "Because he wants to feel the heartbeat of the company. Isolation is a terrible thing for leaders to get used to," she answered.

I didn't understand then; but as I contemplated my big office plan years later, I remembered that day and decided to make one more change. This book isn't about office planning, so I won't go any deeper into this story. Suffice it to say we did open the space and we did eliminate the offices. It wasn't accepted by everyone, and surprisingly, the more junior and middle management leaders were the most upset.

That was years ago, and I've been at a desk in the general population ever since. The changes did create more social discourse, and it made the environment lighter, more friendly. We added games, couches, and white boards everywhere to inspire spontaneous creativity and collaboration. Change isn't easy, but it often is worth the struggle. Stability can be useful, but we cannot let stability become the strategy.

The Seeds of Compliant Behavior

I don't want this to sound like a rant against social normalcy when that normalcy relates to people treating each other with respect, fairness, and grace. We are imperfect beings, and some attempt to channel or restrain our worst impulses makes sense. Instead, I'd like to focus on the restrictions placed by society on our minds. How we think, what we should think, when we should think.

By society, I mean all external influences, from the moment the doctor smacks your butt at birth until now. Your parents, siblings, friends, clergy, teachers, social media, print media, movies, and TV. It also includes the government from your housing association all the way to the Supreme Court of the

United States and everything in between. The social structure we have wrapped around us from the time we are born until the day we die. It is this constrictive imposition on thought that concerns me when I think about creative thought.

We all get a pass on dull thoughts when you consider the billions of dollars spent to make us compliant. Media, entertainment, fashion, food, music—these industries mold opinions, enforce those opinions, and drive us to purchase those options. We grow up with a desire to comply, to belong, to be cool, hip, to be on the inside looking out, because the alternative (we are taught) is a miserable place to be. No wonder it's difficult to think a contrary thought; we never had a chance.

Industries seek stability of intention. They want us to pick them, their products and services; they want us to stay and never leave. Sure, there's competition, but brand and customer loyalty and retention are the key to greater and greater success. Politicians follow the same pattern. Thought leadership is packaged, branded, and sold as a product. An incredible effort is made to keep us in the fold. This social tension is a part of the air we breathe. It doesn't get any better when we walk into the workplace; in fact, it gets worse.

Professionals who've completed advanced education in universities or vocational programs comply with the curriculum as taught. To reject this process or, worse, push back and debate its merits, results in failure to achieve the required credentials to move into the marketplace as a professional. This wasn't always the case. For most of human history, people learned by apprenticing to masters in their craft. There were choices, styles, flavors. You learned through watching, practicing, and eventually mastering the craft; then you adopted an apprentice of your own to continue the tradition.

This was the way people became lawyers in the United States in our early history. A person attached themselves to a lawyer, did menial clerking and research tasks in exchange for the privilege to watch the master. They studied law from books; and when they were deemed ready, they "read" for the law. Of course, there were fewer laws to deal with, and legal proceedings were much less complicated than they are today.

For almost two centuries, the concept of apprenticeship has faded into obscurity in America. Formal education at every level of engagement has ruled the land. However, this is rapidly changing. The old construct is fracturing, apprenticeship is coming back, and the age of free information and online learning is tearing down the ivy-covered edifice of our formal and, yes, *compliant* education infrastructure, one brick at a time.

Why We Need to Break the Chains That Bind Us

The subtitle of this book is provocative for a reason. Bending, breaking, ignoring, and maybe making our own rules is the key to freedom of thought. For what is imagination caged by the constructs of society's control infrastructure, but a beautiful bird starved of light and oxygen? Those who read the subtitle, and feel alarmed are people who live by those contracts. It is their safe haven, their insurance policy in case an unsettled person comes up with a revolutionary idea to change their world. We need to free our minds before we can become creative.

When I was in the Navy, I learned a lot of rules. Structure in the military is reality. Control of behavior is important in an environment filled with heavy machinery, steel walls, floors, and stairwells. There are dangerous weapons, the sea is a dangerous place, rules therefore make sense. At least about physical behaviors. We violated these edicts at our own risk. When it came to thought control, the mechanism was simple and, again, traditional. Only the leaders were allowed to think. Technical experts were allowed to discuss things directly relative to their area of expertise. Gunner's mates did not offer suggestions to RADAR operators or to tactical control officers.

I assume through reading and personal interface with other conventional service veterans that these control mechanisms were similar. That's why being a Navy SEAL was such an incredible experience. Unconventional tasks, planned and executed by unconventional units, comprised of unconventional thinkers. Sure, there were rules, but most of them related to physical behaviors. However, when it came to thinking, we were allowed to be different. I absorbed and thrived in this free-thinking atmosphere. I listened to odd, thoughtful, wild, and wonderous theories about everything associated with special operations. No subject was taboo. I often pondered during my SEAL career if rigid obedience was the enemy of innovative thought.

Chapter Three

How Obedience Impairs Innovation

The smart way to keep people passive and obedient is to strictly limit the spectrum of acceptable opinion, but allow very lively debate within that spectrum.
Noam Chomsky

As I write this book, the United States is in the throes of a debate. This debate, unfortunately, is being held privately and the topic is cancel culture. The idea that one person can express an opinion only to be attacked, shunned, and ridiculed into silence is simply medieval. I hope, like all strange fads and trends, that this too shall pass. However, it illustrates the point of this chapter. When does compliance and obedience go beyond safety and social structure, and become destructive to creative thought?

Cancel culture isn't only happening in politics; it's happening in our workplaces and in our public spaces. Thought is what makes human beings unique. We all have the ability to envision the future, to create fantasy, to mold and bend the physical universe. The human mind is an incredible organ capable of wonder and invention. Shutting it down for any reason must be avoided. Thinking is harmless; it is the actions we take based on thought that deserve moderation and careful consideration.

Historians and archaeologists point out that around eleven thousand years ago humans began to congregate in greater and greater numbers to till the soil, domesticate and raise animals, and build. This early stage of civilization must have required controls of collective and individual behavior. It was less a pact with a strong leader, hunter, warrior, or holy person, but more formal, an imposed set of rules for everything. Eventually these rules were inscribed on tablets to become laws, and courts and judges were established to administer those laws. This was the beginning of large scale thought control.

Of course, early precivilization hunter-gatherers had traditions, rules, and taboos. However, observation of primitive tribes found in Africa, Asia, Central and South America, and in the Arctic seems to show an expression of choice as the basis for social structure instead of hyper-organized methods of control and enforcement. So, why am I wandering down this path? Simple, we all are living and working in an environment of overlapping social control systems. Systems that for the most part influence your thinking and, sometimes, your ability to think freely.

I'm not a psychologist, but for many years I have observed human nature and studied human nature as it relates to planning, executing, and leading. In the last chapter I recalled watching old war movies and noted that several relied on the antihero model, the rebellious warrior, to make a different point. That doing something different to achieve a constructive outcome often is perceived as antisocial, antigovernment, and anti-family. It also is perceived as crazy. Yeah, crazy creative.

Navy SEALs and successful entrepreneurs rely on *crazy* to adapt, evolve, survive, and win. Conventional thinking rarely will get results for two classes of risk takers. Jumping out of a military cargo plane at thirteen thousand feet into a pitch-black night to seek out and engage an armed enemy of the United States is, well, crazy if you think about it. So is leveraging your family's mortgage and tapping out all your credit cards to start or build a business. But are these behaviors really the actions of crazy people?

Obedience becomes destructive when it inhibits free thought. It also becomes destructive when a constructive expression of free thought is seen by authorities as bending, breaking, or ignoring sacred rules. By authority, I mean any person or formal entity dedicated to saying no, regardless of the value of experimentation. Regardless of the potential for innovation or invention. It starts with parents and continues in school. Friends also tell us no. No, you can't be an astronaut; no, you can't be a pop music star; no, you can't be rich, successful, happy, and so on. You get what I'm saying here. You've experienced this firsthand. These *no* messages can be delivered in a light or heavy manner. The naysayers can make you take pause or influence you to abandon your dream completely. What's a dreamer to do?

In my book *Be Visionary: Strategic Leadership in the Age of Optimization*, I highlighted why dreaming was vital to strategic planning. I described a method of assembling the dreamers and the naysayers in your organization to create an effective one-two punch. One team builds a dream into a strategy and the other attempts to shoot holes in their construct. Naysayers can be useful in this context, and I encourage this honest bench testing approach in your organizations. You can take this same path in your own world. Life choices involve deep thought, reflection, vision, and reasoned analysis to test the crazy. Being different is for everybody.

When Being Different Makes Sense

A few years ago, I began a yearlong search for a way to diversify the revenue stream from the company I led as CEO. I handed the "keys" to my chief operations officer and put my weathered money manager hat on. Just like when I managed high-net-worth clients at UBS, I began to analyze my industry for mega trends, opportunities, and eventually, specific companies. I combed through hundreds of business intelligence reports, looked at dozens of pitch books produced by investment bankers selling companies, and even small business broker websites.

The effort steered me gradually to two choices: healthcare or cyber/IT security. These two categories were in ascent and had legs to run. Healthcare was driven by technological advancements and demographics. Especially Baby Boomer demographics. Cyber/IT security was driven by the rise of external threats to data and intellectual property. I had a choice to make. I resolved this dilemma by setting out to meet business leaders in both realms. On one hand, healthcare leaders are dedicated to healing people. On the other hand, cyber warriors are relentlessly focused on stopping bad actors from stealing secrets. The two leadership types couldn't be more different in their approach to execution.

I spoke to dozens of these business leaders and eventually decided healthcare was the more attractive choice. The cyber business space at the time was fractured and disjointed. To thrive there, I would have to be extremely careful and clever. This, in a competitive environment where everyone was cagey and inventive. Healthcare was an edifice, a monolithic, bureaucratic monstrosity of traditions, rules, norms, and an oppressive reluctance to evolve. Healthcare is fueled by federal Medicare and Medicaid dollars, and as a result, has become a mirror reflection of government stagnation.

I began to read everything I could find on healthcare in America. The more I read, the more excited I became. Making a positive difference would be so easy. The performance bar wasn't just low, it was practically lying on the street. I rolled my sleeves up and started to hunt for the company that would strategically diversify my revenue, and provide me and my investors with a platform for dramatic innovation. It took another three months to find that platform and its founder.

The company I found had one employee, the founder. He was an intense personality, but not in an aggressive way. He was a quick thinker, a dreamer, and he was definitely lifting the bar in his healthcare niche. It was clear in my first meeting that the founder had taken the young company as far as he could go. He wanted to deliver exceptional care, not become a financial expert or CEO. He was looking for a buyer who would appreciate and build on his unique model and grow that model.

So, why am I sharing this story? Well, this gentleman was the epitome of a highly effective dreamer who coupled vision with execution. As the sale process continued, I spent long hours at a whiteboard interviewing him and pulling everything I could from his memory about the care delivery model he'd developed. He had nothing on paper, so I converted these interview notes and process sketches into the operating procedures for the company. Most would say this person was different, intelligent but quirky. In this case, quirky was the key to brilliance. We bought the company, and continue to build and grow its influence and impact today.

Obedience and Imagination

I don't want to leave the impression that obedience is evil; it's not. Obedience is a valuable behavior in many situations where a lack of compliance spells disaster. Teaching a child not to touch the stove or poke the power socket with a wire. Getting people out of a burning building or sinking ship. Or as an early phase of military training. Obedience in the military is lampooned by civilians. GI Joe is a brainwashed idiot, who only does what he or she is told and is incapable of independent action or thought. This, of course, is silly and dead wrong.

Nobody would disagree with my fire example. In this scenario, panic and random movement can inhibit evacuation and cost lives. But what about running into the fire? This has been the challenge for military organizations all over the world, since the first group of hunters decided to seek revenge on a neighboring tribe. Going into harm's way isn't natural. Obedience to orders in the military experience starts early to accomplish two key objectives. The first is communications efficiency. The second is efficiency of movement. Thus, giving clear, distinct commands or orders to men and women trained to act, move, or engage a threat in response to those orders achieves a measured result. Even in the chaos and terror of combat.

I was raised by a man who believed in strict obedience and was a compliance guy, at least when it came to kids. My dad was the typical "do as I say, not as I do" sort of disciplinarian. Infractions, even minor ones, never went unnoticed and therefore unpunished. Meanwhile he chain-smoked, drank Old Grandad bourbon, and partied with his country music-loving friends. I grew up walking around on my tiptoes trying to obey or not get caught disobeying. I wasn't the only one in this pickle. All the dads were like this when I grew up. Oddly, this environment stimulated something else in me.

I've since read tales of prisoners of war who sacrificed their physical body to torture and mistreatment, while at the same time creating a different world in their minds. I wasn't a prisoner, but I experienced the same type of escapism. I fantasized about everything, and I read every book I could get my hands on, the stranger the better. This, I believe, is the foundation of my imagination; and my imagination eventually led me to constructive creativity.

Eventually all children leave home and are free of parental influences—good, bad, or indifferent. However, as we all know too well, those early years shape the way we see the world. They mold us and imprint us in a way that's difficult to change. Somehow my escape mechanism saved me from becoming a neurotic obedience freak, terrified to break a rule or color outside the lines. I know I'm fortunate, because I've met and worked with hundreds of professionals who were openly reluctant to test the boundaries for fear of righteous retribution from authority. Even when the consequences were insignificant.

Can these souls be redeemed? Can their fears be addressed and eliminated? I think it's possible or I wouldn't have written this book. I firmly believe you don't have to be insane, a criminal, or a former prisoner of war to start down the path to fearless imagination. You don't have to be a Navy SEAL either. I'll spend a bit more time on the root causes of mediocrity of thought and reactive, programmed fear of change and failure, because it's important for you to face the truth. Once you understand what's holding you back, you will be ready to be different, to think differently.

The Way Out

I moved away from my dad when my parents divorced. I was 14. A strange mix of intellectual rebel, compliant child, and secret agent. I'd become an expert at dodging and confusing my dad's surveillance methods. Evading and avoiding punishment more and more as I grew older. He knew I was doing it. I don't know if it angered him or somehow made him proud. All I know is when I was free of the strict obedience system, my imaginative side was able to step out into the light of day.

Navy SEALs and entrepreneurs have a lot in common. They both face incredible odds. They both put a lot on the line in the hope they will be successful. And they both need to live by using their wits and their instincts. Failure is a part of both worlds, and failure must be seen as a painful stepping stone to eventual victory. If SEALs and entrepreneurs don't think this way, they are doomed.

I've often counseled my sales professionals regarding their fears of facing a large client or prospect. A Microsoft-sized entity seems monolithic, like the Death Star in the movie *Star Wars*. Big, aggressive, powerful, and indifferent to the little companies swarming around their marketplace. Fear of failure is the obstacle; but in truth, the real issue is perspective. There's an old adage related to the fear of powerful individuals: *remember, they put their pants on one leg at a time just like you do.*

In my experience, this works when approaching large organizations. My modification of the adage is: *remember,*

Microsoft is made up of people, and the person you are going to meet is an entrepreneur trying to improve the business position of their team, department, or division. In other words, how do you sell to Microsoft? One human engagement at a time. I truly believe this philosophy. I also believe that managers, leaders, and sales professionals, even people trying to ask an attractive person out on a date, are inhibited by their primal conditioning to respect — even fear — authority and to mitigate risk at any cost.

The notion of establishing a new mindset is tossed around by writers, thought leaders, and media pundits like it's as simple as switching a pair of shoes. I'm here to tell you it is not that easy. The key to breaking out of the obedience trap is possessing the will to try and the discipline to make thinking differently a habit. A habit practiced often enough becomes a demonstration of discipline, and discipline sustained over time reflects a change in mindset. The way out is to embrace this process of intellectual and emotional reform.

I also believe from personal experience that we go through multiple appropriate mindsets as we age, evolve, or face new or interesting challenges. My viewpoint as a new SEAL wasn't the same as when I was a seasoned warrior. The same thing goes for my stint in the finance industry and later in business management. There is no such thing as a perfectly static mental state. Flexibility and adaptability in the face of a changing reality is key here. In the Navy's prisoner of war school known as SERE, you are taught to change your mental perspective to align with your new situation. In a camp where every move you make is observed by guards, where every task is structured, and disobedience results in severe punishment, you have to reset your thinking to survive.

Obedience only becomes destructive when its weight intimidates, reducing or even shutting off free thought, imagination, and the product of imagination: invention and innovation. We must become comfortable with emotionally challenging the status quo, first in our minds and then in our behaviors. Then we need to allow our intellect to disengage from zombie-like conformity to restrictive limits on creativity and *let our minds soar*. You know this is true, you've experienced this; and yet, you may have accepted it as the way things are. You'd be correct. It is the way things are, but it's not the way things have to be.

Willful intellectual disobedience is revolutionary. Exercising this behavior takes courage. Everyone around you will feel threatened. Your actions and words will be perceived as alarming, and your intent will be questioned. Assume at this point that you have a choice; you can be one of many souls shuffling along in a mindless grey crowd of thought servants or be the bright light in that dull mass leading the way to a better tomorrow. You don't have to scream and shout to be effective; nor do you have to randomly challenge everything. Instead, focus your newfound freedom to assess the world around you constructively and pick an area that requires improvement. Being different is about making our world a better place to live and work. Be positive and respectful. Be engaging and deliberate.

It's important to remember that the universe is on your side, a compelling energy wave you need to understand to ride. The universe is in a constant state of change, adaptation, and even reversal. To be blinded by obedience in the face of this natural and immutable law of change is ignorant and, eventually, destructive. To meekly stand by, waiting for someone else to lead the way, is to waste the wonderful mind you've been given. You can start small and work your way into more difficult challenges to address. I'm not talking about charging a machine gun on the battlefield. The stakes are manageable, and the outcomes are open to refinement, but first we must step up. Dare to be different and you align with the universe.

Chapter Four

The Value of Convergent Thinking

When we all think alike, no one thinks very much.
Albert Einstein

Convergent thinking is the opposite of divergent thinking or, put more simply, logical solution design instead of creative solution design. I spent the last two chapters lambasting stability, compliance, and obedience so you could see how they conspire to hold us back, to inhibit free thinking and free actions.

I want to make it clear, however, that convergent or logical thinking isn't a threat to creativity. To the contrary, it would be difficult if not impossible to implement creative ideas without logical construction supporting those ideas like scaffolding. Divergence and convergence are the yin and yang of actionable intelligence.

I've often cited my applicable experiences in the SEAL Teams in my books, and in this case the following illustration fits quite nicely. I described in earlier chapters how SEALs leverage divergent thinking to pull every brain cell into the creative mission planning process. The more impossible the mission, the more creative and innovative SEALs must become.

Convergent thinking, and its associated logical processes, allows the crazy plan to crystalize into a linear series of critical steps along a precise timeline. Resource support for each step along the way must be determined, allocated, staged, and then, at the proper moment, accessed or utilized by the SEALs. Every piece of equipment, every weapon, and every radio must be inspected and confirmed mission-ready, using checklists that follow a predetermined and logical progression.

This holds true for every asset assigned to support the SEAL mission. Ships, planes, helicopters, satellites, quick reaction forces, whatever must work to be successful must be inspected, function checked, and ready for action. It is this combination of creativity and logical planning that makes SEALs and other special operations units so unique and so successful. I've found that entrepreneurs who are successful also are leveraging these two potent methods of thought management. Focusing on all creativity with sloppy execution is a recipe for business failure. The opposite unbalanced approach is equally doomed.

Balance Is the Key

In my books *Be Nimble* and *Be Visionary*, I reflect often on the reality business leaders face when contemplating how they might put my ideas into action in their organizations. Regular people who form the civilian workforce are not the result of a rigorous selection process, at least not as rigorous as the method special operations professionals go through. Business owners, managers, and leaders are at a loss to find dedicated, self-actualized, and self-motivated employees who are loyal to the company and its goals above all else. So how do we proceed?

There are three types of employees. By employees, I mean from the CEO down to the lowest position on the organizational chart. The first type are characterized by positive energy, commitment to a greater good, imagination, and creativity. The second type is dedicated to the task at hand. They possess high standards of personal performance, and, while not particularly creative or excited by change, they know how to get things done. The third type of employee is a blend of the first two types. These are the integrators, the communicators, the arbitrators. They appreciate logic and the brilliance of innovative thinkers. They instinctively understand that a merger should achieve spectacular results. In my opinion, an entrepreneur needs all three in the team to thrive.

Balancing this mix of employee types is the job of a manager when pursuing incremental improvements, or the task of an assigned project leader if the objective end state pushes or pulls the organization to a place outside their comfort zone. This is especially true for crazy, audacious goals. As you might have guessed, you can't treat these three populations the same. You can't communicate with everybody in your organization the same way without confusing one group, scaring another group, or depressing the third group.

I suggest you first recognize each employee type is correct in their own mind. Embrace their commitment to make a stand and figure out a way to leverage all three, instead of forcing them into a mold of your own design. This takes more effort, more touch time, and more listening; but it pays off in the long run. Imagine a team who all thought the same way. Cohesion would be a given, messaging simple, and all emotions would operate in sync. The danger in this utopian fantasy is channeled group think. You need diversity of thought to bring out the best ideas. You need intellectual friction to become excellent.

Maintaining balance also means creating a work environment where people feel comfortable speaking their mind without risk of retribution. Now, I'm speaking of positive thoughts here, constructive insights shared openly so everyone on the team can absorb tangential points of view. A melting pot of professional inputs, logic, dreams, and concepts all swirling around, forming the very air you breathe. In an organization led this way, it becomes easier to leverage the balance of views to push beyond opinions on the status quo to a more enlightened and refreshing framing of the possible … the way things *can* be.

Diversity of Thought

Diversity of thought is not thinking differently, at least not in the context of this book or my thesis on how SEALs and entrepreneurs get results, despite the rules. Diversity of thought is having different points of reference or views that add color and depth to a team's engagement. For example, I've practiced this many times over the years by bringing a diverse group of dissimilar professionals into a project or mission planning process.

When I arrived at SEAL Delivery Team Two in Virginia Beach, Virginia, I wasn't an expert on the Navy's mini submarine. Nor was I acquainted with the large, floodable, garage-sized shelter the minisub rode in on the back of fast-attack and ballistic submarines. I was in awe of the technology both represented, but soon discovered the population of the specialized command was split down the middle. SEALs on one side and Navy deep sea divers on the other.

The floodable shelter, called the DDS, was operated by experts in deep diving. The Navy's divers were elite in their own right, selected for both routine operations and, in this case, special ones, too. After a few weeks of observing this situation and speaking with experts on both sides, I began to create a new unit, a task unit three times bigger than the old version. And one more thing—I decided to fully integrate the Navy divers as warriors.

If you can figure out complex dive tables and are courageous enough to risk your life on deep dark dives in the unforgiving ocean, then you probably are going to be fine learning how to carry a weapon, drive raiding craft, and operate tactical radios. By cross-training the divers in all things SEAL, I forged a bond between the two groups. A bond of mutual respect, and more, a brotherhood. The task unit was the first of its kind related to the technology we employed, but in retrospect it's this merging and fusing together of two elite and diverse groups that I see as my greatest accomplishment. The very fact that the divers were not SEALs injected oblique objectivity into the planning process, making us stronger not weaker.

In another example, years later as CEO, I was dismayed at the attrition I was seeing in our accounting and finance group. A revolving door of recruited, vetted, and trained professionals, installed and then gone in less than a year. Time and time again I pleaded with the chief financial officer to fix the problem and watched in consternation as he acted like nothing was wrong. This was a case where the expert was blinded by their expertise and their experience, not empowered by it. After two years of hearing excuses and theories, I decided to shake things up a bit.

The tenure of my other, non-financial employees averaged four years in a company seven years old. Most of my operational leadership team were elite former military. Marines, SEALs, Bomb Disposal, and Rangers. All had advanced degrees and were adept in motivational leadership. I chose one person for my intrusive experiment—a retired sniper and multiple tour combat veteran, he was six foot two and weighed 250 pounds. Not your typical accountant profile.

My guidance was simple: you are not an expert in financial operations, but you are an expert on leading people through crazy. Jump into their processes, their meetings, and especially look at their recruiting to onboarding approach. Do this for a few months; then we'll talk. A few interesting things came from this experiment. First, my SEAL sniper gained empathy for the vital role the finance folks played in our collective business success. Second, he recognized that the senior leaders, however credentialed and experienced, were not instinctive. They were so linear and process-oriented that their human engagement skills were shoved in the back seat, rarely applied on a day-to-day basis.

Based on his observations and recommendations, we changed things. I placed this sniper in the hiring and onboarding process to act as a counterbalance to the finance leaders' points of view on hiring. He also had veto authority on hiring bonuses (there were none), salaries (the leadership believed in negotiating low starting compensation), and training (the practice before this was to plant the newcomer in a cubicle and order them to execute). In the end, we stabilized the shop for a few years, and the diversity of two methodologies produced a more effective team.

Convergent Thinking and Process Development

In the finance team example, we also conducted a spirited lean six sigma walkthrough of every finance and accounting process step, and evaluated every supporting system. My SEAL sniper (with an MBA from George Mason University, by the way) led this broad investigation, because the team was terrible at communicating among themselves and with their two finance leaders.

On the surface everything looked okay, but my sniper with the MBA noticed the team members were taking long breaks in pairs to walk around outside the building. He eventually discovered these were therapeutic gripe sessions. Of course, according to the chief financial officer, everyone was happy. As we began our six-sigma process analysis, we realized we needed to act as a communications bridge between the accountants and their senior leaders.

Oddly enough, these specialists who relied desperately on systems and processes were apparently incapable of agreeing with each other on what to do. Crazy, right? Answering the question *what to do* is the very definition of process development. A six-foot-two mentor and facilitator made the six-sigma exercise fruitful, but it shouldn't have been that difficult.

In my book *Be Visionary*, I describe how to use the naysayers in an organization to punch holes in the conceptual plan developed by the "dream team." I also make the case that while optimization isn't an effective substitute for strategy, it is needed once a strategy and the support plan to achieve that strategy are defined and set in motion. Convergent or logical thinking also is a binary partner to divergent or different thinking. To do one without the other would be meaningless. To do both in concert just might change the world.

My story about the accountants bears this out. We spent days pulling the current logic or illogic of each critical path in the finance and accounting realm until we had each one documented. Right or wrong, we had all the process steps in plain sight. Then we brought everybody back in to address these crime sketches. It was ugly and beautiful at the same time. In short order, steps were evaluated by the entire team and accepted, dropped, or edited until complete. Then, collectively, we moved to the next major process chain and again until we'd corrected the logic of the entirety. Convergent thinking has this powerful effect.

When to Break a Few Eggs

Now wait. Isn't the subtitle of this book all about defying the rules to get results? Well, yes and no. At this point I trust you are beginning to see the subtle interplay between crazy and logic. Without logic, crazy is, well, crazy. With logic, crazy is impactful. A logical study of rules should reveal weakness in their construct. They are dated, based only on tradition, the view of a single person, the view of a crowd, missing the point, not effective, and on and on. This is where you can apply the will to bend or break the existing rules and create more valuable controls or toss them out altogether. Logical analysis followed by enlightened and open-minded thinking. An effective one-two punch.

The challenge here is my reference to the three types of employees concept raised earlier. Most people are stuck in a mind rut, unable to see and recognize the beauty of the fine woodgrain as they sweep the floor. Unable to recognize the value of logic as a partner to creativity. As an individual, you need to ponder which kind of person you are right now and decide if you are willing to shift into the middle category, seeing the forest and the trees in each situation.

Absolutism feels powerful, but it narrows the mind. Consider your status and your end goal for mindful behavior and make the move, or stand pat. The decision is yours to make, but now you know there is a choice. If you are a leader, this is a more challenging decision; but you can offset your personal choice by surrounding yourself with people who think differently.

Imagine a team of diverse specialists that is constructed to have an equal measure of the three employee types as I defined them. Dock workers, crane operators, marketing executives, a few junior accountants, all brought together by elegant design to generate a different outcome for the organization. Insight at so many levels, empowered to think, to speak their mind. Facilitation is key to positive and constructive management of this gaggle of diversity, a light touch that guides the collective stream of consciousness toward an unknown conclusion, one that surprises the facilitator as much as the team involved.

Speaking of teams, the SEALs are referred to by their members and alumni simply as the Teams or, in more recent history, the brotherhood. My experience with that organization and the team concept contrasts sharply with how teams are created and managed outside the military. A committee of representatives is not a team. A committee of diverse representatives is not a brain trust of creative world changers. A committee is just that, a committee; each representative focused on their constituency's objective, not the common good.

Now before you decide to disagree with me, apply this simple test. A team and its members share the same fate ... if they lose or if they win. SEALs die or are wounded; professional teams win or lose together. Does a committee share this same experience? If a team that is really a committee fails or wins, does it, in your experience, suffer a penalty or reward together? Equally? I'd venture a guess your answer is no. A true team, especially a team assembled to solve a big challenge, needs to have skin in the game. The members need to focus on the team winning, not their department. If you are embracing the wrong sort of team, then break the ineffective and frankly misleading paradigm and start afresh.

Convergent thinking can be leveraged to ensure your irregular or unconventional workaround is set up for success. Sure, bend or break the rules, but be a builder not a destroyer. Reset the new normal and lock it in until it's time to blow it all up again. I know people who are so enamored of being a change agent that they forget the second part of the exercise. It makes no sense to be in a constant state of change, never establishing the foundation to execute in a different way. This is where dynamic thinkers would be well served by teaming with an engineering mind, someone who knows how to apply organizational design principles to lock in the thought gains.

All this change stuff can be exhilarating as well as exhausting. Be mindful of the challenges and tasks involved and build a team of both divergent architects and convergent builders. If you are rational and ethical, then you know how your drive to reshape things will destabilize and alarm everyone around you. If you break it, you own it, so be thoughtful, constructive, have fun, take risks, and keep thinking!

Chapter Five

How Conditioning Inhibits Free Thought

When your mind is full of assumptions, conclusions, and beliefs, it has no penetration, it just repeats past impressions.
Sadhguru

Personal history can and will affect your self-esteem, your acceptance of change, and your willingness to take risks. The history I'm referring to is the scrambled collection of memories, perceptions, methods, formulas, traditions, cultural norms, pain, and joy that you carry around with you every day. This bubbling hot soup of mixed messages represents your self-image, and that self-image can be a difficult bear to wrestle.

Why are some people confident and others reluctant? Why are some people able to roll with life's punches, while others are knocked flat by a mild tap? Americans spend billions of dollars each year on books, streaming and downloaded instructional courses, therapy, and even drugs in an effort to moderate or control the negative ramifications of poor self-image. Huge sums of money also are spent trying to achieve supermodel physical proportions for the same purpose.

Reminding people that they are less than they can be and have less than they could have is a blood sport in America. We are bombarded with technology-enabled, psychologically fine-tuned messages, designed in marketing laboratories to convince us we are messed up. Once this messaging takes hold, the messengers are only happy to show us the easy way to correct the problem.

As a business professional, I understand that creating a need, real or imagined, and making that need feel urgent sells. As a father, a husband, and a leader, I also understand we are collectively absorbing an incredible amount of focused, coordinated, and funded negative input at the same time. These influences on our thought and behaviors may not rise to the level of laws, formal rules, and cultural traditions, but they are just as powerful, maybe more so.

Some Baggage Is Real

Don't misunderstand. I realize trauma is a real thing; and for many people trauma at an early age, or at an early stage in their lives, can be overwhelmingly defining. I was able to transcend my childhood by taking one of two paths offered by an uncaring universe. One path led to self-destruction and the other to self-development. I made my choice to go down the second path, but it wasn't easy. Many of my friends were in the same situation as me and they chose differently. It took many of them years to crawl back to the positive path. A few didn't make it.

The term baggage is used here in the common application: stuff me, you, we all carry around in our heads. When used in society, baggage is assumed to be negative memories, imprints from our parents, our general upbringing, or maybe trauma that was more impactful in its effect and lasting damage. Sometimes the baggage that inhibits our ability to see and think freely isn't bad. Positive memories play a part in how we see ourselves, too.

How can positive baggage have negative connotations? It's easy. Imagine a kid raised in a wealthy home. Life is simple. You want, you get. Style, grooming, and travel are all a natural part of your existence; and the expectation or feeling that your world reflects the real world is a given. You go to special schools surrounded by people just like you—enabled, enriched, and secure in your belief that this is what life is all about.

There are two scenarios where this type of psychological baggage causes problems down the road. The first is continued affluence. If you've never failed to achieve a desire, a goal, then you will have a self-image that on the outside appears healthy.

However, placed in a difficult situation where the challenge requires tenacity, courage, and creativity, it may be hard to understand why someone else hasn't solved it for you. This use of your brain wasn't required growing up, not where risk of failure has serious and costly ramifications.

Here's another way to understand what I'm saying. When I was a SEAL training instructor in the basic or selection course, we observed a curious phenomenon. This strange occurrence played out repeatedly, class after class. Star professional and collegiate athletes, even elite endurance Ironman Triathlon competitors, quit during physical events. Too cold, too tired, too stressed by the nonstop flow of challenges.

It was strange to see, but eventually we came up with a theory. Put simply, these high-end athletes had never failed physically. They were therefore mentally ill-equipped to handle the situation. They'd always outperformed everybody, starting at a very young age. More importantly, their self-image didn't have room for athletic failure. They didn't have time to learn how to cope with this new self-image.

Meanwhile, all around them were regular guys. Guys who trained for months just to pass the basic exercise test at the start of the grueling six-month course. Every run, swim, obstacle course event was misery. Every single day. They were used to being below average or just average athletes. The difference was they knew that and could deal with it when physical failure loomed large.

When a top three finisher of the famous Hawaiian Ironman Triathlon quit on a mile-long bay swim, everyone was stunned. The Navy went so far as to investigate the circumstances. How could an incredible athlete, trained to swim two-plus miles in the ocean, bike ride 112 miles across scorching hot fields of lava rock, and finish with a marathon run, all performed one right after the other, quit on a one-mile swim on a sunny morning in Coronado, California? The investigation went nowhere, leaving many on the outside of the SEAL Teams scratching their heads. Positive baggage can be just as debilitating as the negative stuff, maybe worse.

The second scenario, where this affluence can have negative outcomes, is when that profusion ends abruptly. This scenario has been portrayed in books, movies, and television episodes for years. It's found in Greek plays; Shakespeare eloquently addressed this all-too-human fall from grace. It's the riches to rags three-act play; only when it's real and it's you, it sucks. I mentioned coping. We learn to manage through trial and error. No trial, no error, no coping mechanism. It's as simple as that. Left at age 15, 18, or 22 without the means to live and no idea how to take that first step toward self-reliance.

Some Baggage Is Borrowed

I'm not an accountant. However, over the years I've employed at least 40 of these specialists. Anyone familiar with my books knows I put a great emphasis on teamwork, a collaborative culture, cross-training to build resilience, and leadership accountability. I'm agnostic when applying these principles; however, I've repeatedly been stymied by this unique brand of professional. Accountants appear to love stability, embrace sameness, and prefer when their job is precisely spelled out. No deviations. I logically understand this behavior, but I try to influence my accountants to evolve into participating change agents. It hasn't worked so far.

These are salt of the earth types, hardworking people whose personalities are attracted to the regimen of math and spreadsheets. These professionals love to solve problems when the numbers don't tie out. They relentlessly chew on the anomaly until victorious. After many conversations, I realized the more senior and experienced the accountant, the more damaged their faith in change. To many, change for them has meant termination, reductions in force by the new owner or new leadership. For this population, accepting and rolling with change is not only contrary to their nature, it's terrifying. As Mr. "Let's change to improve," I'm terrifying, too.

It's not just accountants. Many other business professionals have suffered through the same bad change management experiences in the past. Before they even hear or read the words announcing new initiatives, they react, a form of post-traumatic stress syndrome, or PTSD, taking over their minds. As a leader, I'd love to pull everybody together in a big huddle and toss the gauntlet down in front of them. "Here, this is the challenge!" Just once I'd like to see them collectively cheer, roll up their metaphorical sleeves, and say, "Bring it on!" But this doesn't happen, at least not unanimously.

This is the normal state of affairs. The very mention of change excites twenty percent, confuses twenty percent, and terrifies sixty percent. This is what I call borrowed baggage. The fears these folks have are borrowed, not related so much to their core psychology, but a result of learned behavior through professional experience. Change an accountant's duties or where they sit, and there's a fifty-fifty chance they're looking for a more "stable" work environment the next day. What can we do to make them comfortable? To make them open to unconventional thought processes?

Love, Kindness, and Mentorship

You don't have to be a psychiatrist to understand how personal and professional baggage holds back creative thinking. Though most of this book is all about how to be creative, I want to take a moment here to express how we can all help each other to evolve beyond these mental inhibitors. Love is the first condition required. If you are incapable of loving your fellow human beings, then there's more going on than I can address in a simple book. This form of love is about decency, empathy, sympathy, and a willingness to help. It must be real to be effective; and trust me, *it is effective.*

Loving each other isn't about physical love or emotional love. It's about the core social contract we should all live by. This contract isn't written down, per se, but it's obvious in many societies through demonstration. By aiding an injured person on the sidewalk or providing food and shelter directly or indirectly through donations for those in need. Or maybe just listening with empathy. These are all expressions of love. Throughout human history, from primitive tribes to great nations, a social contract of human behavior based on protecting each other and the common good marked successful cultures.

In ancient times, the concept of tribal affiliation, national pride, or citizenship with duties embodied this social covenant. In later centuries, cultures attempted to codify these benevolent behaviors in law, often influenced by religious mores, habits, and attitudes. A modern workplace is no less a human environment than a village. How we treat each other is within our control, and showing love as I've described can make a positive difference.

Imagine how hard it would be in an office to bully coworkers if everyone felt love for each other. Bullies expect positive results from their behavior—advantage, influence, power, or social authority. If we don't grant bullies these things by not tolerating their attack on those we love, the bully shrivels up and fades away. In an atmosphere of mutual love, it is okay to voice a crazy idea without risk of retaliation or ridicule. Love opens the door, empowering each of us to dump the baggage.

Kindness is the observable symptom of love. Nurturing or supporting each other doesn't mean we have to agree intellectually. It means we are prepared to act in a civil and positive way to assist each other when needed. In a business, any organization, this behavior should be seen across the spectrum of work and from the top down. It is what people feel when they visit a group with a strong positive culture. It is observable, palatable. It feels good just to be near this type of atmosphere.

Expressions of kindness can be nearly insignificant, or they can be significant. Across my businesses, we send flowers to mark births and deaths. We call sick or hospitalized employees to check in on them. Several times over the years we've kept employees on the payroll for as much as a year to maintain their health benefits while they fought cancer, too weak from the curative process to come to work. We don't do these things because there is a payback expected. In the example of our employees' cancer cases, only one of three ever returned to work again. We did, and still do these things, because we love each other; and that means kindness toward each other is a given.

Mentorship makes sense if you care about the people in your organization. Taking the time to offer insight, acting as a sounding board for ideas, or simply listening is a gift. There are far more informal mentor relationships than formal ones. Mentoring is truly an act of kindness, and it's highly effective in teasing out the creative person inside all of us. The baggage sits there like a weight on our shoulders. It's there when we wake up and when we go to sleep at night. This baggage is attached to our conscious and subconscious mind. Love, kindness, and mentoring are only a few ways we can collectively help each other to strip away the baggage one chunk at a time.

Why an Expert Mindset Impairs Innovation

We've all interacted with a know-it-all. The corporate expert, the neighbor who's been around for 40 years, the overeducated blowhard in every party. Expertise is like science—it's fragile and fleeting. The universe is in a state of continuous change, making anything static, especially thought, moot in no time. In the first chapter we discussed stability. Seeking and protecting stability of thought is a way of locking down specific expertise, corporate memory, formulas, rules, laws, or traditions to ensure those empowered by this status quo remain empowered. This is a different kind of baggage, but no less limiting.

Scientific theory requires rigor. That rigor is to be applied to collecting raw observed data and then testing that data to determine the truth. In 1932, near the town of Clovis, New Mexico, finely made spear tips were unearthed. The find was between twelve and thirteen thousand years old. The oldest proof of human presence in North America. From that point to around 2016, the Clovis theory of human migration and expansion in North America was held as a sacred truth in archeology. Until 2016, any scientific paper, speech, or book testing this premise was ridiculed and shunned by mainstream science. Then something strange happened in the Carolinas.

In 2016, an archeologist wondered what might be under the ground, deeper than the Clovis period in our early history. He knew it was a silly idea; the scientific community was firm that there was no archaeological value in digging deeper. However, this archeologist *did go deeper*, and what he found sparked a firestorm of controversy. He found evidence of a habitation. A people older than the Clovis people, their spear tips less refined. These unnamed humans had found the area near the joining of two rivers to be advantageous, as had every human from their time to the present. The artifacts were dated ten thousand years earlier than the findings in New Mexico.

A few years later, while digging to extend a highway near Los Angeles, California, the project was abruptly halted upon the discovery of mammoth bones. A paleontologist was called in and his discovery shocked his scientific peers. The bones were dated to at least twice the age of the Clovis spear points. This wasn't the crazy part. The bones showed tool marks indicating humans were extracting bone marrow for food. The immediate reaction by the scientific community was predictable. The case for how and when human migration into America occurred had been made decades earlier. It was proven science. The discoverers in California were shunned and ridiculed by the experts. A universally closed-minded collection of academics, who had dutifully memorized the story as taught in their degree programs. They waved their hands, laughing, and saying there is nothing to see here!

More recently, other discoveries in North America have confirmed how much we don't know about our ancestral past. It's okay to be skeptical. Skepticism is healthy. Test the data, create the hypothesis, and prove the hypothesis. If true, change the rules, the history, the knowledge. Be open to the outcome, even if it radically alters the status quo. Of course, a love of stability combined with human nature makes being intellectually curious feel like risk-taking behavior. Understand that; then ignore the impulse to hide in the shadows. Listen to experts, but test. If you are an expert, then listen, observe, measure, test, and accept, even if that means changing the status quo — *your status quo!*

Chapter Six

Incrementalism

Incrementalism is innovation's worst enemy.
Nicholas Negroponte

When searching for the right title for this chapter, I pondered the message I wanted to convey. I personally live in both the present and the future. It's the way my brain is designed, or maybe I learned to think this way when I was a teenager and my world was being ripped apart by my parents' divorce. Thinking about both my immediate survival and a better future became my core operating mode. Later, joining the Navy was less a deliberate act than an escape plan. This approach to life has helped me illuminate the potential for better times ahead and revealed incredible opportunities over the course of my life.

I've always been a student and observer of history, eventually buying into the adage that history tends to repeat itself. However, I think that it's true, because human behavior tends to repeat; and that in turn, seems to be the driver of history's cyclical nature. We are what we are and always have been. Curious, closed-minded, violent, peaceful, both selfish and selfless. Sounds confusing, right? How can we persevere in changing the world using the bright light of discovery if it's doomed to be doused in the next inevitable cycle of human ignorance? Remember, they were called the Dark Ages for a reason.

One thought I have is that our tendency to be risk adverse results in us watering down our drive to explore, to radically change the way things are. We dodge or hide from threats, rather than confronting and defeating them. Our feeble strategy is to modify our existence only slightly, tweak things a bit, but only a bit. Moderation in all things. Like snails, we attempt to cross the four-lane highway a centimeter at a time, never reaching the other side. This is incrementalism and it sucks. Posturing, preparing, warming up, stretching out, only to take one small step forward. It's ludicrous when you think about it, yet many of us do this as individuals, organizations, nations, and as a species. There's got to be a better way.

When Incrementalism Works

In the SEAL Teams, we practice something referred to as baby steps. It's incrementalism applied to physical activity or mental activity, usually training people in complex skills, but it's also used in mission planning. The distinction between baby steps and wild leaps of insight is akin to the synergistic convergent, divergent relationship noted in a previous chapter. The two methods should coexist, working in concert, relying on each other to produce better balanced outcomes.

It's hard to imagine a martial arts instructor holding out a solid piece of wood and demanding the new student to break that board with a spinning round kick. It takes a long time to teach that physical skill, and just as long to train the student's mind to be comfortable violently striking a hard object. Ever tried to break a thick piece of planking with your hand or foot? I've watched ten-year-olds line up to break boards and observed their facial expressions. Most, if not all, approach the exercise with enthusiasm. Then, one by one, they make a mental decision that determines success or failure. Trust me, there's a powerful mental aspect to performing this trick successfully that requires progressive acceptance of what defines success and the price of that success.

From a thought perspective, baby steps fall into the convergent category. There may be only one way to teach the spinning back kick, or to rank order the incremental training process a student should perform, or there may be many. Logic, however, does come into play when planning out the course of instruction. In situations where you need to implement change, to materialize creative thought like convergent thinking, incremental planning is a key to building the future. Now I really have you confused. I told you incrementalism sucks; and as creative or innovative strategy, it does. But it has a part to play.

A special operations mission follows a two-step methodology. First, you have the creative planning session. Like a garage band jamming and experimenting to find the right mix of music, SEALs throw ideas at each other, test those ideas, and then accept or reject some or all of those ideas. This creative brainstorming is applied to each mission phase in progressive order. How do we move from the safe base to the bad guy's border? How do we move from the border to the target? How do we move from the target to the border? How do we get home? Once the creative part is locked down, the details are hammered out, phase-by-phase.

Second is execution, described as a step-by-step plan to reach your stated objective. Most experienced special operators will tell you few plans survive reality. Weather, mechanical issues, and timing of key events change frequently, making a mess of the elegant mission plan. I've personally lived this reality in the military and in business. In my experience, the more complicated the plan, the more fragile that plan is in execution. Oh, and I forgot to add the enemy, or in business, the competition. Your opponents also have something to say about how well your plan works.

Plans that are developed using flexibility and simplicity will survive reality. Over time I learned this rule. Our two-part planning process only worked if our special operators performed the plan in a way that allowed for adjustment and modification during execution. We adhered to incremental analysis to define the risks and possibilities, then launched into the mission doing the best we could to follow the script. However, when our assumptions and conditions on target began to deteriorate or evaporate, we still had our creativity. Adapt, improvise, win.

Untethered Thought

If you think of our brains as highly capable calculators or extraordinary storage devices, it makes perfect sense for you to embrace memorization, rote learning, and linear or logical thinking as the way to leverage your mind. While the brain certainly can do these things, according to medical science it's apparently not the true design intent. The advances in our knowledge related to human brain functionality are amazing! Science also is revealing that many of our widely held beliefs and traditional academic theories about how our brain operates are suspect, if not outright false.

Centuries ago, the academic world in Europe embraced the premise that information must be delivered by experts, then absorbed, memorized, and upon command, regurgitated to the teacher or professor by students. Not much has changed, despite our advanced understanding of how the brain works. Schools and universities still follow this methodology. Brain science has grown in sophistication as technology has grown to allow us to observe the brain in action. Contrary to the medieval point of view, the highest and best use for the human brain is to connect information and construct thoughts. These thoughts can be dreams, questions, answers, insights, and much, much, more. We are missing out if we only continue to use this wonderful organ as a library.

When I explained why social or systemic restrictions of thought contribute to our risk avoidance programming, I failed to mention how the way we learn is also a contributor to our ignorance. Rote memorization and mindless reading without debate, critical thinking, or creative expression, is an insidious process that dumbs us down. This approach does not use the brain as designed or expand our mental ability. In fact, these techniques numb the mind and subtly reduce the risk that we might shake things up with our unruly and provocative ideas. Teachers tolerate expression and creativity in elementary school—nobody takes a six-year-old seriously—but by the time puberty arrives, teachers begin to push back on wandering minds.

Getting into trouble for daydreaming is a good example of this. Rather than curiously asking what a student was thinking about, they are admonished and told to stop. Tying down free thought, one class and one year at a time. No wonder it's so hard to get adult professionals to loosen up and comfortably participate in brainstorming. They are reluctant without knowing why.

The brain is certainly a learning machine; I know that is true. It also is a thinking machine. The chaotic way the brain pulls and tosses chemical signals here and there to arrive at conclusions isn't linear, and it's wonderful. Carl Sagan, the famous twentieth century astronomer and writer, was asked to assist a NASA project. His task was to envision how an alien mind might operate. He was flattered by the assignment, but realized he didn't even understand how the human brain worked. He began to do research.

In 1977, Carl Sagan published *The Dragons of Eden*. His thesis was based on his intense study to understand how the human mind is designed to work. His research surprised him. He found that we are all misusing this wonderful tool. He documented much of what I've referred to, the centuries old mythology that the brain was a storehouse. Later research illuminated the true purpose of the brain's elegant design, categorizing our higher brain functions into task-focused, analytical, and explorative discovery.

So, how do we use this information? How do we learn to shift from one higher function to the other? In later chapters I'll provide answers to those questions; but for now my goal is to get you to loosen up a bit ... to relax and set aside the to-do lists, the Key Performance Indicator (KPI) dashboard, and stop problem solving. Just for a little while. I want you to think about each of the barriers to free thought I've described. Obedience, compliance, personal and borrowed baggage, and then concentrate on stepping out of the cage they create in your mind. Untether your thoughts and let them roam free. This is only the beginning.

Most Opportunities Only Come Around Once

In my early professional life, I didn't have the faith or confidence to make bold moves. Especially in business. Oh sure, I wasn't afraid of jumping out of a plane at thirteen thousand feet at night or driving a minisub in pitch-black water under an aircraft carrier, but that was another life. That level of confidence was due to a long and painful learning curve. When I left the Navy, I soon realized my courage and confidence was lacking. I wasn't experienced in my next vocation, and taking things slow and easy was safe.

For the first two years as a money manager and then again during the first few years as a business division vice president, I hedged. I planned small, performed small, and achieved unimpressive results. At some point in each of these examples, I realized what I was doing and made a concerted effort to change course. That's when things accelerated. Looking back as I write this, I wonder why I had to repeatedly reestablish my confidence. How many opportunities did I miss as I risk-mitigated my way through the initial stages of each career change?

At the time, it didn't feel like I was being a wimp. In fact, it usually felt like I was performing on the edge of acceptable outcomes. Of course, that "edge" was a well-established boundary put in place by all the other risk-averse people I worked with and for. As a rule, I tend to beat myself up for small behavior faults and don't judge myself by how my peers are doing. If I'd looked around during those first couple of years, I'd have realized that, even with hesitation and risk avoidance, I was still performing well based on the standards. Did I waste time wringing my hands over each step forward? Yes, I did. So, what shook me free of this incrementalism and fear of failure?

In each career path, the epiphany—the turning point—was different, but also the same. As an aspiring money manager, I arrived at a moment when I realized I wasn't an employee. I was a business owner. Instead of the sales numbers acting as my guide, I realized I needed a long-term strategy. This literally came to me in a flash of insight. Sitting at my desk staring at a screen displaying my weekly, monthly, and quarterly sales production results and the variance to targets, I realized I was working my ass off for the numbers and not much else of value.

That shift from measured production element to business owner was profound. I was responsible for finding and signing clients, gathering their investable assets, and putting those assets in motion. I was charged personally for almost everything—business cards, brochures, etc., all except the office space and computer. I managed the relationships, and lived and died by client retention and client growth. As a business owner, I also was responsible for the future. I sat down and started charting my path and thinking about what I really wanted to achieve. It was uplifting and rejuvenating. After two years of drone-like effort, I was transformed.

Sales professionals know what I'm talking about when I say sales management is heavily influenced by micromanagement and micro measurement of incremental inputs to achieve equally incremental outputs. It isn't about having a plan to take over the entire territory after 24 months. It's about repetition of sales techniques and methods executed with discipline every day. The philosophy is: input effort by the numbers (calls, appointments, etc.) drives output numbers (sales, referrals, etc.).

As noted at the beginning of this chapter, there is a place for baby steps, for incremental analysis or execution. I just don't believe it has a place when we need to envision and implement bold, heroic course changes. This book is about breaking out from conventional thought processes to see the forest *and* the trees. To practice ways to shrug off the constraints and restrictions of thought imposed on us by all the external and internal influences, the mental handcuffs we all carry around with us. Don't think small. In truth, opportunity exposes itself in flashes of understanding or acute awareness. It takes practiced sensitivity to pick up on its subtlety and courage to seize the moment before it is gone. And gone it will be if you hesitate or second guess yourself.

Incrementalism and Processes

I'll make a clear distinction here between my definition of incrementalism applied to creative thought and the use of processes. Processes are useful in defining workflow. They identify key or critical steps in a sequence from start to finish. They show an interface with other upstream or downstream workflows, and they can be used to diagnose problems. An explosion in the use of formal processes occurred right after World War Two in the United States. Flush with victory over two foes, the United States had become the world's most efficient and prolific producer-manufacturer of military weapons and platforms.

During the four years of World War Two, the United States produced 297,000 combat aircraft, 193,000 artillery pieces, 86,000 tanks, 2,000,000 tactical vehicles, and 5500 ships. We also created methods and management techniques that allowed for this incredible productivity. Soon after the war, this capability was converted into making refrigerators, appliances, and cars for America and the world. Planning and execution for effective, large-scale, linear production relies on organized process workflows that evolved into a science during World War Two. These approaches transformed the way we did everything, including non-manufacturing-related business operations.

When I joined the SEAL Teams, we were using US Army planning tools to create mission presentations. These formats and templates were by design easy to understand and to the point. However, by the early 1980s, SEAL missions were getting more and more complicated. We stopped using the Army tools and shifted to linear, phase process diagramming of our missions. Each aspect of the mission, from start to finish, was further defined by a long list of micro steps supporting the successful completion of each phase in the operation. In a short time, we'd gone from a five-paragraph format for planning to a method that generated hundreds of phases, tasks, and subtasks.

At first this was a boon for the SEALs. It was much better at finding critical nodes of risk and identifying resource needs, refining the attention spent on even the smallest of items. The rub here was soon apparent, at least to the old-school Vietnam SEAL veterans. They were used to keeping it simple and creative. The more our senior leaders fell in love with the hyper-detailed process approach, the more compliant we became to the model. The process itself became the objective of the planning exercise, not a tool for creative planning.

Incrementalism is comfortable. It can become the main operating system of a person or an organization, taking the place of free and unencumbered thought. Why take the time or risk failure by breaking out of the established pattern? What does a person or an organization gain by ignoring conventional controls and workflows, by leaping forward, sideways, or jumping straight up? Incrementalism, baby steps, and workflow processes have their place in life and in business, but they should never be relied on for forward-looking creative and innovative exploration. Think big, think boldly, be different!

Chapter Seven

Revolutionary Thinking

Emancipate yourselves from mental slavery,
None but ourselves can free our minds!
Bob Marley

I guess I'm one who believes if you're going to upset the applecart, then why not go big? If you believe, as I do, that incrementalism makes it inevitable you will lose the race, why not push for revolutionary change? This idea is exciting and compelling, especially to people frustrated with the status quo, in life or in business. Revolutions can be exhilarating, and they also can be destructive, despite how altruistic or pure the objective.

During the early years of my career in the SEAL Teams, there was a shift from a monolithic jungle-focused, counterinsurgency role to multiple appointments and responsibilities. These new positions involved operating environments other than the jungle, where SEALs made their name. The intent was to make these strategic changes slowly, to make the transition evolutionary. That's not what happened. Speed of execution converted evolution into revolution.

Speed creates its own special dynamic. I've come to a position where I believe speeding up thought, design, and implementation carries with it a sense of urgent purpose. I believe it is this awareness that excites and challenges people to cast off convention and delve into the art of the possible with rigor. People tend to drift if given all the time in the world to think or to plan. They don't viscerally feel the drive to act. They may spend years dedicated to deliberate planning and development as lethargy reigns and the world leapfrogs past without glancing back.

History's Lessons

Revolution appears to be spontaneous throughout human history; but if examined closely, the seeds of dramatic change were sown long before the streets filled with people screaming for change. Revolutions are usually violent, aimed initially at destroying the status quo before settling down to rebuild in accordance with the new point of view. This isn't always the case though. In 1989, the empire of the Soviet Union fell, along with its vassal states, in a bloodless revolution of incredible significance.

All revolutions begin with thinking differently. Since most of us are not interested in changing the course of nations, let's stick with what we can impact: our personal lives, the lives of our families, our professional trajectory, and our organizations, if we occupy positions of leadership. Those four categories are more than enough to work through. Brain power applied to our daily challenges and frustrations can move the needle slowly or quickly, depending on how we lay the groundwork for change.

The onus is on us to transform first. We need to acknowledge the restrictions on our minds and make a distinct effort to clear all the baggage out of the way so we can get to work. Revolutions can be small and personal, or much larger in scale; but they should always be driven to make things better, not to gain power and prestige. People tend to see power as a right, or status, when real power is a responsibility. A truly powerful person is changing everything around them by the purity of their intentions, making the world a safer, happier, more interesting place.

Intellectual Humility—The First Step

This chapter is about improving outcomes in a bigger way. Revolution in thought is still subject to influences that blind us to the clarity and insights new data provides. As a first step in my process, you need to be able to clear your active mind of your daily to-do list, step away from the key performance indicator dashboard, and get ready to be as open-minded as possible. Intellectual humility is all about creating a blank slate to write on, and not about leveraging education, past best practices, or formulas.

Another aspect of this first step is setting aside the positive and negative emotions of our past. For example, when you've had a string of wins you tend to be more aggressive and less mindful. You rely on what has worked to solve the next challenge instead of absorbing the immediate reality. On the flip side, if you've suffered a string of failures, you may become reticent and shy away from risk. Both distort the way you think, decide, and lead. You can't truly be clear-minded and thoughtful with either condition rampaging in your head.

I suffered the downside of being overly confident on a combat mission. I was on a roll. I'd planned and led 20 or so missions and felt that my team of SEALs and I were in the zone. Everything clicked and we could do no wrong. My men were happy to have a leader who seemed almost lucky in his planning decisions. It couldn't get any better. One day we received a mission tasking to hunt down and capture a senior enemy intelligence officer. It was an important operation, and lots of people would be monitoring the entire process. I was ready.

We coordinated with aerial surveillance, helicopter gun support, a large mobile response force of Army infantry, and selected a Navy patrol boat for our insertion method. At nine o'clock in the evening, we eased two large rubber boats, referred to as CRRCs, over the deck of the patrol boat and into the water. The boats were heavy, filled with soft fuel bladders, extra outboard engines, and six SEALs per boat. After traveling a quarter mile toward the beach, we hit what we thought was a sandbar. It wasn't. Instead, we'd hit a mudbank hiding just three feet under water.

This was the beginning of a terrible mission, at least from the standpoint of planning. It felt like the world was watching us as we got out of the boats and began carrying and dragging them to the beach, four hundred meters away. The tide swing was 18 feet, and we'd caught it going out to sea quickly. After three hours of mud, we arrived on the beach exhausted. It didn't end there. We entered a mangrove swamp as planned, but eventually had to ditch the boats and start wading through the inky darkness.

Navigation systems were notoriously inaccurate in third world countries back then, and I was soon hopelessly lost. I decided at three in the morning to turn 90 degrees to the left and find a way out of the swamp. An hour and a half later we exited the swamp and found ourselves on a road heading inland. That was the good news. The bad news was we were looking at the ocean. I'd led my team in a grueling four-and-a-half-hour loop through the swamp to arrive near the point we'd originally landed.

We'd planned to hit the compound where the high-value target was staying precisely at five thirty in the morning, just before sunrise. Standing there while the sound of the nearby waves mocked my arrogance, I was at a loss as to what to do next. My team and I were beyond spent. We each carried 80 pounds of mission gear: bullets, radios, and weapons. We were coated in dark, sticky mud, adding another ten pounds or so in weight. My chief eased up to me after a few minutes and leaned in close. "What's the call, boss?"

Mr. Wizard didn't have a plan. I was still shocked at the utter stupidity of my collective leadership mistakes. My confidence was further impacted by the gravity of the mission. It was critical we nab this guy in less than 60 minutes. I cleared my mind, took a deep breath, and absorbed the reality of where we were. The road looked like it headed inland, but what if it didn't? What if it banked left, away from the swamp paralleling the beach? My chief was waiting, my men were waiting, and a lot of other people waiting and watching.

"We're going up this road. A point man and machine gunner paired in front, 20 to 30 feet ahead of the rest of us. Staggered file formation. Oh yeah, pass the word that we're running." We had 40 minutes left in the timeline. Running was what I said we'd do, but it was more of a shuffling jog. At 5:29 in the morning, my point element stopped. They'd found a low fence. It was the target compound.

Afterwards we handed the bad guy to the Army and took our bows. The infantry guys thought we were cool, mud and all. Just another high-performance special operations mission in the books. I knew better. Then my chief pulled me aside. The sun was getting hotter, and the blue sky seemed to make all my self-doubt go away. Sure, it was rough, but we'd completed the task. "Sir, we left the CRRCs back in the middle of the mangrove swamp." I sighed and wiped a bit of mud from the face of my watch; my worst mission wasn't over yet.

I usually spend more time emphasizing intellectual humility, because it is what grounds us and allows us to think clearly. Without this first step it's difficult to impossible to perform the next two. Most successful people appear confident, and many are bombastic characters. But I'm willing to bet they are breakthrough artists in their fields because they've figured out a way to ignore the past and get humble. Humble people are hungry people, and hungry people wake up every day paranoid they don't know enough or haven't done enough to outthink the competition. Be humble and allow the insights in.

Intellectual Curiosity — The Second Step

Now that your mind is clear of distractions, especially fear of failure or arrogance, you are ready to seek out fresh perspectives. This is a fun exercise if you approach it in the spirit it represents. Don't cull information; instead roam freely. Start with strangers in your business or industry and then branch out further. Read, listen, and speak to the odd, the improbable, the crazy, and soak it all in. This is how we begin to break free of group think, as well as "me think."

Curiosity isn't about research in the mode of an analyst or grad student. It's about searching everywhere. It's about letting these new insights and ideas into your head without any reservation or screening. You already know how to reduce the flow of information so you can do that exercise later when you're all charged up with delightfully new angles of thought. This is hard for most people. We've all been conditioned to apply what we've been taught, to use what we've learned or experienced to date. This is a trap, if your goal is to break free from the mundane. Take a chance; you might be surprised at the way the world looks from a new and different point of view.

I do this as a mindset now; after several years of starts and stops, my freewheeling stroll through the world of information and ideas has become a continuum of curiosity. I look at all sources, all industries, all people first before asking my company's experts, my personal brain trust, to tackle a challenge. Be curious and you'll never go back to the been there, done that mentality.

Intellectual Creativity — The Third Step

Okay, so you've performed the first and second steps and are ready to experience the payoff. This exercise prepares me for both planned and unplanned innovation engagement. Engaging in solution design, writ small and simple or significant and complicated in scope. By thinking this way, every day, my intellectual humility allows me to be curious, and that curiosity prepares my mind to achieve extraordinary outcomes.

Creativity without these first two steps is often stale and simply a cheaply painted version of old mindsets, resting on old assumptions, and limited by old rules. True creativity relies on humility and curiosity, so we can solve problems, create new processes, innovate products and services, or invent startling new ways to succeed. This level of creativity naturally resides in children, the naïve, and the uninitiated. This is because they don't have prerecorded and practiced perceptions, formulas, and ruts they've dug with that overvalued shovel called experience.

It's no fluke that most of the world's scientific and geographic discoveries were achieved by people younger than 30 years old. The same holds true for many of history's military geniuses and political revolutionaries. Here's an eye-opener: James Monroe was 18 when America declared war against Great Britain. Alexander Hamilton was 21, and James Madison was 25. Albert Einstein was 26 when he discovered the theory of relativity. Alexander the Great conquered the known world before the age of 30, and Napoleon Bonaparte rose to the rank of general by the age of 24. Soon after he became leader of the French Republic.

The ignorance of youth is its secret weapon when creativity is the objective. My three steps help anyone at any age to position themselves in an intellectual state that closely replicates this youthful bliss, rendering you free of the burden of knowing what can't be accomplished, and ready to embrace the true expression of enlightened thought. Intellectual creativity is a mature game, but it doesn't have to be stodgy or burdened with dead weight. The challenges of life are often serious with consequences in lost jobs, lost treasure, or even survivability. Try these steps and make it a habit. Before long it will become a mindset, and you will surprise yourself and others with your enlightened openness.

Wonder, Awe, and Spectacular Outcomes

Believe it or not, embracing the reality I paint in the first few chapters by itself could be enough to open your mind and change your world. Like addicts, it's a significant emotional breakthrough to admit there is a problem; and that addiction is adherence to silly rules, outdated procedures, defunct processes, flawed systems, and worn-out traditions. I can't emphasize enough how this restricted method of seeing the world limits successful outcomes for all of us as individuals, professionals, and leaders of organizations. Shed the chains, open your mental aperture. Do this and you are more than halfway to being different.

I wrote about the visionary mindset in my second book *Be Visionary* and noted that the young have the easy, almost effortless ability to dream and see the wonder of our universe. As we age, we don't lose the capacity or ability to do these things; we simply succumb to the world's insistence that we grow up. Dreaming and having a sense of awe may be seen as childish in the adult world, but that doesn't mean we can't learn how to think young again. Being young is a state of mind. Don't believe me? How many 35-year-olds do you know who walk, talk, think, and act like they're 60? There are many examples of 60-year-olds competing in challenging sports, reading a hundred books a year, and learning new languages. Your choice—behave the way you feel or behave the way you're capable of feeling.

The human brain can handle the drive to reignite youth. Unless affected by disease, the brain is ready, willing, and able to operate across all its many and wondrous functions. You are likely the reason your brain may not be firing on all cylinders. You crimp down on its capabilities by adopting minimalist thinking processes. I'm speaking of all manner of personal and professional habits. Have you ever met someone who was proud to tell you they'd never read a book after graduating school? Do you know anyone who always defaults to the playbook, the approved guidance, or the standard operating procedures to answer a question or solve a problem? That's an atrophied and woefully underutilized brain hiding in plain sight.

I'll say this again. Unless disease is involved, we all are capable of firing up our brains to full power again. The mechanism in our brains that scientists call the forager switch isn't disabled when we reach puberty, graduate from school, or get married. It lives in all of us, intact, ready to be exercised. The other switch, the task-focused mechanism, is overstimulated and sadly used to devise the future, one extension of the measured past at a time. It's time to get physical, to bend or break the rules blocking our way to dramatic, even spectacular results. Let's go!

Chapter Eight

How to Bend the Rules

You don't learn to walk by following rules. You learn by doing, and by falling over.
Sir Richard Branson

Here's the thing. We know most rules are in place to protect us, to guide us, and to inform us. I think of rules as mental constructs designed forthrightly or in error, based on fact and logic or not, and always framed for the time and context in which they were created.

When I was a kid, we weren't allowed in the house until mealtimes. We were expected to stay out of our parents' way and play in the fresh air, for hours. It was the universal parent rule and it worked. Then came sketchy vans and child abductions, and soon those days were over. The rules changed.

When I was a SEAL, the rules changed all the time. Bad guys couldn't be shot unless they were in uniform. Soon the bad guys ditched the uniforms and kept shooting at us, so the rules changed. Vehicles loaded with explosives were devastating our military. These bad guys had shaved heads, acted alone, and were between the ages of 18 and 35. Pretty soon they knew that we knew that, so they started attacking us with two guys instead of one, hair and all.

Eventually they switched to a man and a woman in the front seat. Then families with kids. All willing to blow themselves up for a cause. The rules for engaging this threat changed every week. At some point in this process, we were being asked to break other long-held rules for conduct and behavior. Americans don't grow up believing it's okay to hurt a woman or a child, let alone shoot them. In Iraq, we were faced with rules layered on rules, entangled and complex.

Luckily, most of you don't have to deal with this level of ethical and moral pondering. That is unless you are a doctor, nurse, emergency medical technician, fireman, or in law enforcement. These professionals on the front lines of our society face these rules-based dilemmas every day. No, for most people the stakes are less onerous; and the choices, between right and wrong, good and bad, are less nuanced. Business can test that statement, however; greed can twist a person's sense of integrity to the breaking point.

When I speak about breaking rules in the context of creativity, I mean breaking the rigidity of your thought process. Please do follow all the laws, regulations, and rules set up to protect us and those we love. These are a part of what we call civilization. The absence of these types of restrictions is the very definition of chaos and anarchy, and I mean the evil and destructive kind. We are focusing on the rules, written and unwritten, formally taught or informally absorbed over time, which clog up our cognitive functions, limit our intellectual horizons, and stymie discovery. Let's get started.

How Navy SEALs Bend Reality

As a young student in the six-month-long SEAL selection course, I was taught that to cheat was a punishable offense. Given the well-deserved reputation of the course, my fellow students and I toed the line. Sure, we cut a few corners here or there, but nothing dramatic. Then I arrived at SEAL Team Two. The command was full of seasoned combat veterans. Old by the time they hit their mid-thirties, these men were full of stories and wisdom. Practical, applicable wisdom to be sure, and that included bending the rules.

For these heroes, getting the job done and getting back alive was the objective. The missions were challenging, sometimes nearly impossible at first glance, yet they persevered time and time again. Their method was straightforward: do the unexpected, learn the rules of the game from the bad guy's perspective, and then use their rules against them by violating those expectations. So, we dressed up like anything other than a movie cliché Navy SEAL, traveled in average cars instead of military vehicles, and borrowed people's homes as safe places in the heart of the enemy's turf.

In exercise play, the bad guys were American infantry, either Army soldiers or Marines. They all wanted to bag a SEAL, so they broke the rules, too. If we were told there were ten people on target, there would be 40 when we arrived. If we were told the area was quiet, we would see every road intersection and bridge manned with guards, sweeping flashlights everywhere and even hiding with night-vision devices in the trees.

In one of my first major military exercises as a new SEAL, our leaders explained this to us. Then they elaborated on how we were going to deal with the reindeer games being played by the opposing force. The plan was simple. We would jump into a swampy area and jog for six hours to reach the target two days ahead of schedule. Our task was to place multiple fake bombs in a small building representing an enemy headquarters. The opposing force units would normally deploy a few hours before dark on the day we were supposed to do our mission. So, when they showed up, in this case 20, instead of the two guards we were told to expect, the bombs were already in the building.

My officer waited until midnight and then sent the radio call to the higher authority that the mission was a success. We were long gone, by the way, far outside the reach of the enemy forces. The exercise control center communicated to the opposing force that the mission was successfully completed. Of course, the "bad guys" denied the target had been attacked. Eventually they were asked to search the inside of the building; the rest became a part of the SEAL mythology. Ninjas at work.

We changed the rules to counter the reality of our adversary's mindset. This happened over and over again until I learned how to bend the rules to win on the battlefield.

This example may seem like cheating, but it wasn't. Instead, we were exercising our right as unconventional warriors to think our way through challenges. To sweep down, guns blazing, and toss fake explosives inside the building was always an option, but a conventional one at best. We all understood that the most powerful weapon we had was sitting right between our ears, so we leveraged our brain power every mission.

How Entrepreneurs Bend Reality

Leading a commercial enterprise for the first time provided a series of eye-opening moments. In the military, at least in the special operations world, and when managing people's money, I'd witnessed apathy and risk avoidance from time to time, but nothing like being in the corporate environment. As a SEAL, you spend most of your time with other SEALs, so it was a real shock when I saw superiors, peers, and subordinates all seek protection against change and the risk change represented to them. It was almost a part of their DNA, their core operating system. So, imagine my surprise when almost every idea that came out of my mouth was squashed.

There's a saying in the military that, "It's better to beg for forgiveness than to ask for permission." This became my mantra in the early days of corporate leadership. I wasn't entirely alone, though. In a large institution, I found kindred spirits, other business rebels quietly scheming to make things better despite the environment. I'd read about entrepreneurs, met entrepreneurs, and managed money for them, too. Now I was conspiring with them at the ground level. It was tense and then exhilarating. My newfound friends coached me on how to act, to report, and how to win small battles. I was on my way!

The first rule of being a business rebel in a larger organization is to map out the players. Who's watching and waiting to catch a rulebreaker? Who's in authority who will covertly assist the rebel cause? Who can you trust with your plan? I'm from Nebraska, and usually straightforward and honest in my communications. This was a mistake in this atmosphere. I had to treat it like a SEAL mission. Gather intelligence, study the human terrain, and plan carefully to succeed.

Success is the key. Solve a modest problem in an unconventional way, and you'll be applauded even as you are chastised for bending rules. Do this often enough to create a positive track record, and some bosses will make a self-serving decision to turn a blind eye to your irritating insights, as long as you keep winning. Fail once and you will be on your own without allies. Success in this way creates another situation I wasn't prepared for, envy and resentment.

Your peers are those aligned with you on an organizational chart. They are also your competitors in the commercial world. Every movie cliché about backstabbing and cutthroat tactics is very real, and it was all around me. Not when I wasn't being effective, only when I started winning. These peer competitors didn't necessarily announce their animosity to my success, so I learned the hard way that working out or chatting in the hallway might provide insights into my methods and projects that could be used against me. These accusations bubbled up to the leaders, and they began to form opinions about me without knowing me at all. Meanwhile, I naïvely blundered about, trying to initiate improvements large and small, totally clueless, at least in the beginning.

I figured it out eventually. I was getting upset and felt betrayed. Of course, this was because I was comparing my new world to my old one. I wasn't bending or breaking laws, governmental regulations, nor was I doing anything unethical or immoral. My crime was seeing a mess and cleaning it up. In hindsight, it makes perfect sense. Human nature is consistent and easy to observe. If ten workers are told to work for eight hours making widgets, and worker number six makes ten percent more widgets a day than his or her peers, well I think you know how this plays out. Rather than step up and increase widget production across the team, the team communicates to number six to knock it off. "You're making us look bad!"

I believe entrepreneurism should be the philosophy at every level of business, regardless of its scale. If this was the case, medium and large corporations would be bounding forward continuously, challenging their competitors with better ways to do everything. I needed to mature and accept that leaders and others would not leap at every idea that came out of my mouth. Eventually I became better at reading the room and controlling my delivery. I was appreciated rather than avoided and soon began to be promoted, rapidly moving to the position of senior vice president in three years. Did I fail? Of course, I did. But because I tried to make things better every day, my successes far outnumbered those failures; and my evolution as a communicator, combined with a creative mindset, made acceptance and advancement possible.

Small business owners are assumed to be free-range thinkers, experimenting and challenging the laws of business physics daily. Alas, this isn't always the case. Case in point, the former big company technical or business person decides to start their own business. They go to friends, colleagues, books, podcasts, even the small business association, looking for ideas, plans, insights. Then they borrow money and start their operation.

Here are a few issues right out of the box. First, formal business plans and advice or personal knowledge derived from larger companies immediately saddle the freshly-minted entrepreneur with a lot of conventional baggage. Instead of thinking like a simple lemonade stand to start, these excited small business owners try to replicate the wrong paradigm. At this level of play, you don't need to think about rules when it comes to strategy and planning, sales and marketing. You are free to improvise, get instant positive or negative feedback, and try, try, try again. More on this in later chapters, but the point here is to enjoy your freedom. Breathe in and experience the new business for a while, and let the truth impress and guide you to success, one epiphany at a time.

If You're the Boss

When you're in charge, you can evaluate the rules imposed on your direct reports. I suggest you do this if you just assumed the position or have been in place for years. Rules tend to have a shelf life, and regular reviews help clean out the attic, so to speak. I'd begin with the serious rules. You'd be amazed at how many key compliance actions are no longer in line with new laws and directives. They become stale and then void, putting your organization at risk.

The second phase of a leader review should be about decision making. Are the presentations too formal, too stilted, too packed with data that they lose their energy? Is the process inclusive or exclusive? Are ideas and insights sought from all corners of the organization or does it look like an episode of *Star Trek*, with the top three calling all the shots? If your decision-making rules are stuffy and restrictive, you're probably flying half blind, with much of the embedded experience and knowledge of your organization ignored.

Next, address communications. Are they open and fluid, or channeled and stovepiped? Do your managers encourage inputs, insights, ideas, innovations, or even inventions? Or do they choke off all that brain power based on titles? How do alerts, alarms, criticisms, and warnings get passed throughout the organization? Can employees directly approach management and start a conversation, or must they get permission? These may seem like random things to evaluate, but communication is the key to better, more timely information; and in some cases it's the key to minimizing damage.

Then consider damage control processes, solution design methods, problem solving approaches, and crisis management. Again, are these functions and scenarios hyper-managed and exclusive, or do they rely on an all-hands-on-deck game plan? Considering the other evaluations areas already covered, do they improve the situation or inhibit full awareness by everyone with the capability to contribute to a successful outcome?

Now it's time to look at the lower-tier rules, norms, and traditions. Many of these controls fall into the category of workplace environment. Does your organization reward seniority by physically segregating the winners from the little people? Do the minions have to travel to the leadership floor of the building to seek an audience or are their leaders accessible and open to being approached? Is the space an open-concept design or an endless field of cubicles? Is there an inviting and comfortable break area? Are employees allowed to take quality breaks or do supervisors stare at them, tapping their foot as soon as they arrive at the coffee machine? Atmosphere counts.

There are many more rules in most organizations—some are tenure-based, some are based on seniority, and others are just there. As the person in charge, you can have an incredibly positive impact just by addressing the burdensome pile of restrictions and biased perks that are strangling creativity, freedom of thought, and inspiration. You have the authority to water down, remove, minimize, and modify all these control and management mechanisms; and you should do so, immediately.

I noted in an earlier chapter that we all carry personal mental baggage, and we all borrow inhibiting baggage from other people and professional environments after we enter the working world. Do your part to decrease the negative effect of this second form of mental restraint. Get your people, your team, your department, division, or company to focus on the clarity of purpose they need. Provide them with an environment that is stimulating, not stifling. One that is inspiring and exciting, not one that is based on blind compliance and subordination to tradition or rank. You have the power to be the first one to bend the rules in pursuit of the greater good!

Chapter Nine

How to Break the Rules

There are no rules. That is how art is born, how breakthroughs happen. Go against the rules or ignore the rules. That is what invention is about.
Helen Frankenthaler

There are many clever quotes and maxims about rules and rule breaking. One that rings true to me refers to a master being one who knows the rules before breaking them. I'll not rant on for another chapter about the effect of rules on spontaneity, cleverness, cognitive agility, or all that stuff. Instead, I want to discuss when and why we should be willing to break, instead of just bend, a rule.

Most rules are in place for a reason. That word, reason, is the key to understanding the validity of a rule. It is the sensibility and intelligence one might, or should, apply to making a rule that is likely to affect many other people. Reason is a great word, and it is often tarred as not reflecting emotion or passion. I don't believe this is so. Reason isn't pure cold logic. It is, in my opinion, the sum of one's considered position, all things considered, logic and emotion included.

So, we'll start with the assumption of good and noble intentions. That means we need to understand the rules and, if possible, the person, persons, or institutions that created them. Context is key to understanding as well. If you're still not sure what I'm alluding to, think of the endless debate over the meaning and words in our American Constitution. Since we can't interview the original drafters of that document, we are left with their journals, articles, and interviews, all slanted by a cultural and technological divide.

Pay Homage to the Rules First!

The first and second steps in my three-step process are intellectual humility and intellectual curiosity. To hold to these faithfully, we must agree that rules, until evaluated and studied, cannot be condemned out of hand. Part of this approach is to set aside what I've been harping on in the first part of this book. Knowing how rules can inhibit free thought, we must set that philosophy aside for a moment so we can honestly and clearly look at the rules.

As you know by now, this sets us up to be genuinely curious. So, I want you to do your homework. Take the rule, or rules, you are interested in breaking and hold it up, study it, and figure out why it exists. In my experience, I surprise myself when I do this exercise the correct way. A rule that is a clear obstacle to progress and enlightenment begins to make sense. If I cheat and color my process with prior opinions about rules in general, or stop my inspection before it's complete, I'm setting myself up for problems. Don't cheat!

When I started looking for an acquisition a few years ago, I wasn't an expert in ninety-nine percent of the industries I studied. I was looking for sustainable margins; and by sustainable, I mean margins that were driven by a long-term trend, with multiple years of runway into the future. Healthcare is where I landed, and I was immediately struck by the restrictive nature of the industry. There were lots of laws and regulations, to be sure, but there also were a ton of cultural norms, traditions, habits, and simply weird practices that mystified me.

Setting aside the laws and regulatory mess for a moment, let's chat about the rest of the barriers to excellence I found in healthcare. The first one I should have understood already. The physician is royalty, and his or her castle is guarded. I thought it was only the doctors I'd used over the years. But no, it is a universal thing. You can't see the doctor for any reason, unless they give permission and then only on their terms as to subject, location, and duration. Imagine running a restaurant or a gas station like that! The buyer is not calling any of the shots.

As an entrepreneur, this irked me to no end. It wasn't a personality trait; it was a control mechanism, and it was universal. No capitalism in play here. No letting the market decide. There wasn't even a way to determine who the best of breed was before you made your potentially life-changing decision. Just show up at the scheduled time and do what you're told. Oh yeah and pay through the nose for the privilege. Alas, it turns out this rule has legitimate origins, and it is more a reflection of society and consumerism than the medical community.

A hundred years ago people lived in town and either walked to the doctor's office or sent a message to the doctor to visit their home. The doctor's time was parsed out according to the need; and as towns grew, they attracted more doctors. We didn't know as much about the human body either. Moms and grandmothers were knowledgeable in many basic first aid and medical treatments, and could set bones, stitch cuts, and deliver babies. As the twentieth century matured, so did the science of medicine. The more we learned, the sicker we thought we were ... and with issues and diseases that mom couldn't cure.

Don't get me wrong—medical science is wonderful. I had my kidney cancer surgically removed with a remotely guided robot in 2017. Advancements in medicine have been dizzying, so much so that the need for medical professionals, treatments, pharmaceuticals, and care centers has grown astronomically. Gone are the simple days when mom sent a child down the street to fetch the doc. We are overwhelmed with calamitous possibilities, and there aren't enough trained professionals to go around.

The first thing that had to change was compensation. The second was access. A doctor's time became increasingly precious, and that put pressure on costs associated with seeing a professional. Supply and demand also kicked in, and that's really the origin of the castle keep mentality. Triage is the process of sorting out medical issues from most critical to least critical. Access control started as triage and ended up as optimization of a doctor's limited amount of time. It's evolved into a cultural norm, a tradition, a hard and fast rule, all wrapped up together.

My journey of understanding made me aware why the access rules existed. Until I could find an alternative process that delivered professional, qualified, optimized care in some other manner, I was stuck, like all of us, with these rules. Imagine if I'd barged in, all CEO like, and just changed everything! I still hate the way this is done in medicine today, but it is a set of rules I must live with for now.

At Last, a Bad Rule!

Okay, you've chosen which rules are in the way, you've honestly appraised their true value, and eureka! You found a rule that needs to disappear. What does that rule look like? In the context of being and thinking differently, the rule should clearly obstruct those goals and not legitimately be a critical requirement to operate going forward. As I write this book, one notable example is the post COVID-19 lockdown debate about bringing people back into the physical workplace.

Apart from work that absolutely must be performed in a physical space (factory production is an example), rules related to this debate seem more about tradition than effectiveness. Consider this nugget: if work productivity for knowledge workers didn't falter during the forced lockdown virtual experience, how does physical presence in the workplace have anything to do with effectiveness? Here's a reason—trust.

Traditional thought regarding worker effectiveness has always really been about worker productivity. It irks traditionally-minded leaders that remote workers might be finishing all their assigned tasks in three hours instead of six and using the surplus time Monday through Friday to play.

In a weird twist of logic, these "productivity scientists" would rather have them doing tasks the old-fashioned way, expanding three hours of work into a full workday. Silly, but this is the current debate.

Using this example, how does the 2019 office rule regarding physical presence, standards for work attire, lunch and break time rules, size of cubicle or office allocations, and so on apply today? How do any of these rules contribute to high-performance execution of assigned work? Of the many loud criticisms of virtual or remote work I've heard or read, only one resonates with me as far as creativity is concerned, and that is emotional collaboration.

Emotional collaboration is the direct and physical interaction between people the way human biology intended, face-to-face and in person. As amazing as remote visual conferencing has become, it has an emotional flaw. People participate displaying their game face. They know every little tic, twitch, and grimace is being closely observed. In person, this self-awareness on-screen melts away, allowing people to read their fellow employee's thoughts through facial tells and body language.

The in-person employee also is free to modulate their voice as they interact, another very human way to convey information. When we are together in a room, we focus on the speaker, but we also scan the room for reactions to that speaker. With their guard down, the listeners display reactions, and those reactions are a form of group communication. So how do we get rid of these rules, yet retain this one awesome part of true human interaction and the resulting outcomes?

In a sense, solving the remote versus in-office conflict is a struggle more based on emotional attachment to the past than intellectual analysis of merit. It does, however, demonstrate the difficulties one encounters when longstanding rules are changed or eliminated. As a CEO, I chose to assess the type of work my people performed, then asked them through a survey in early 2021 if they would prefer remote or in-office when COVID-19 concerns waned. Only two percent chose in-office work. I read the room and downsized office space over the next 24 months by seventy percent. Two years later, we've survived the pandemic and tossed aside the in-office tradition.

In the SEALs, we were suspected of routinely breaking rules; but as noted in the last chapter, in practice we more often bent or ignored them. Here's an example of a rule we broke and for good reason. Projectile weapons have been around since the first ancient human threw a rock at wild game or a human adversary. As technology advanced through the millennia, the art of aiming a projectile weapon was a critical element of martial training. In the late 1970s through early 1980s, terrorist attacks by organized believers became a threat to world stability.

In 1980, the British Special Air Service, or SAS, resolved a terrorist crisis in London, rescuing hostages held by five Iranian gunmen. This event was televised, and it accelerated the development of hostage rescue and counterterrorist units across the globe. In the SEALs, we were focused on jungle warfare and just beginning to develop Arctic warfare and combat diving skills. Creating a viable maritime counterterror unit was the next new capability. As we trained and learned, both from mistakes and successes from other units in Europe and in Israel, we realized we had to change the way we thought about small arms use, especially the art of aiming.

The rule forever, if you wanted to make sure your shot was accurate, had been to assume a stable stance (there were only two choices), close one eye, focus on the sights, and then squeeze the trigger. As we applied these age-old techniques, we soon realized we needed to break all those rules and start over. Hostage rescue work requires commandos to execute precision shots in crazy conditions and unstable surfaces, aiming at only a small sliver of a target, without hitting the hostage. Another problem was seeing an entire room as you entered and started shooting. Closing one eye made you tactically blind to half the situation.

So, we learned how to shoot all our weapons with both eyes open, applying the same high standards of tactical shooting accuracy. We had to learn how to shoot those same precision shots from any angle, foot placement, balanced and unbalanced. We practiced climbing ropes and taking shots, swaying in the wind. We practiced with gas masks on, and in low-light or no-light conditions. We used night-vision goggles and so on. In retrospect, the days of standing on a 25-meter range, legs spread and planted firmly, arms extended to form a triangle as we squinted and fired seemed silly. However, this was the way marksmanship had been taught and practiced since the dawn of firearms. These collective rules and traditions failed the assessment test, a test based on a new reality. They had to die an honorable death.

Break, or Break and Replace?

As you may have noted in that last example, the SEALS replaced the old rules with new ones. Albeit these new rules for precision shooting in a combat, specifically in a hostage rescue, context were more fluid and relied on adaptability instead of conformity. I explained in earlier chapters that rules are not inherently evil. They have a role to play in constructing an ordered and focused reality. If they hold up over time, if they pass honest assessment and scrutiny, so be it! If they don't, then maybe it's time to eliminate or replace those dinosaurs.

I like to pay homage to the Hippocratic oath when considering change to rules—first do no harm. Now, this may seem like risk mitigation, and in a softer application, it is. It would be foolish to rampage through an organization breaking rules and traditions just to show how radical or bold you are. I always encourage my leaders to be thoughtful when creating or modifying an organizational chart. There are always good intentions and there are always unintended consequences.

When it comes to organizational design, the brain power applied should be akin to an NFL coach rethinking their offensive plays. Test, experiment, ponder, test again. Do this on a laptop, a white board, or a piece of paper; don't act on your construct using live stunt dummies (your employees). In a way, when changing an organizational chart, every single change affects a multitude of rules and traditions. The chart may look easy to understand before you fiddle around with it; but in truth, most human structures do not align with the published plan.

The larger the organization, the more this is true. Real interactions, if tracked, traced, and discovered, would depict something more like an ant farm. The wiggly racks going here and there represent the informal communications and authority that are *actually performed* every day. The workarounds, the collaborators, the friends who listen, the connectors, the naysayers, the power hungry, and those reluctant to exercise power. All scrambled up in a bowl, simmering just below the surface.

Now here's something scary—you think by changing a section of the chart, swapping out leaders, enforcing new rules for working together, that this new normal will really happen. These are just a few of the land mines waiting for you when you decide to change things up. Here's the good news: if you take the time to study the ant farm, then you just might see how to leverage *that* structure to achieve your audacious goals.

If you're inclined to break a few eggs, make sure you clean up your mess and leave the folks with a better paradigm. In the precision shooting example, the old was eliminated and replaced with the new. In the example about remote work, you need to understand your workflow, your talent, and their attitudes toward remote or in-office work structures. Then make the changes, rewriting the old rules. In these examples, the new approach reflects the new reality. Remember, though, once the new rules are in place, watch your reality like a hawk. If it dances off into a new place, then observe, assess, change.

I'm using a new way to look at building business plans. It's based on the book *Back of the Napkin to Business Plan in 11 Slides*, published in 2023 by the incredibly successful thought leader and businessman extraordinaire, Brandon White. Brandon has a long history of raising capital as an entrepreneur, experiencing over one hundred venture capital pitch sessions as he started, grew, and sold two great companies. Brandon then became an executive responsible for managing the assets of a multi-million dollar family foundation. This time he was on the other side of the table, listening to the ideas pitched by people seeking investments and grants.

In speaking with Brandon as he developed the thesis for his book, I asked him why he decided to make it so brief in page count and so simplistic in design. His response was wonderful. He was aware of the business school standard formatting that for decades represented the bar when creating a business plan. He also was aware of the more stilted version of that standard demanded by banks before they approved loans. And he has lived the life of a businessman. His personal and professional experience told him that the reality wasn't in sync with the traditional methods of explaining a business.

Brandon went with his heart and his mind, structuring an elegant and succinct, step-by-step approach to understanding your business and explaining it to others, all in 11 PowerPoint slides. All critical points, no slop, no jargon, no need to get an A for effort based on page count. It changed the way I build business plans today. It is a new paradigm based on the existing paradigm and not some stuffy college textbook from the 1970s. If you break the rules, *make things better!*

Chapter Ten

How to Ignore the Rules

There are no rules. That is how art is born, how breakthroughs happen. Go against the rules or ignore the rules. That is what invention is about.
Helen Frankenthaler

Think about this crazy idea. Freeing your mind to roam, to be wowed, to investigate and interrogate the world doesn't violate anything. Not one rule or tradition. Not a single regulation, ordinance, or cultural norm. That's because thinking isn't regulated; acting is. Acting based on thoughts that run afoul of the established structure of controls—benign, appropriate, or outdated—is having an impact on reality. Until you do this, you are free to laugh and dance in the playground of your inquisitive mind.

This means that once you've successfully purged or set aside the conditioning that's holding you back, you can turn your mind into a wonderous laboratory of innovation. In a later chapter I'll delve into how to accomplish this in a practical and constructive manner, but for now, I want you to relax. We've discussed bending and breaking obstructive rules that prevent creativity and progress. Now we are going to chat about when to ignore the rules.

Ethics

I've decided for the purpose of illustration to separate ethics from morality for the moment. The standard dictionary definition of ethics incorporates the concept of ethics as a broad, mutual understanding agreement regarding conduct. I'll leverage that by adding that it is also the specific concept, written or unwritten, a person is expected to adhere to if they are to practice a profession that requires defined conduct, both good and bad. I did not add religious elements to my statement for a reason, and will cover this in the next section on morality.

Let's start with the general application first; society agrees in general on proper and improper conduct. Many of the practical rules, rules that stand up to intellectual scrutiny, relate to this general code of societal ethics. Here's an example. There are rules prohibiting jaywalking in most cities and for good reasons. The rules of traffic flow at an authorized speed conflict with freedom of pedestrian movement. If jaywalking wasn't a thing, anybody could walk out in front of a moving vehicle. The result would almost always be vehicle 1, pedestrian 0.

In the early days of motor vehicles, this became a crisis in America's cities. The problem had existed since the dawn of metropolitan development. Horses, chariots, carriages, and other large objects were running over pedestrians. But it was in the early twentieth century when city leaders decided to regulate the freedom of pedestrian movement for their own protection.

It was a balancing act, to be sure. The traffic had to move at a slower regulated speed and stop at crosswalks. Stop signs and eventually stop lights further reduced speed, and in combination these rules radically reduced pedestrian injury and death. Of course, this was all about the motor vehicle and therefore didn't change pedestrian behavior sufficiently. That's when jaywalking rules were imposed. Now the ethical playing field was set. As a citizen driving or walking in the city, you were obligated to play by the rules. If you did not, then you would pay the consequences. Great solution, right?

So, let's say you're walking down the city sidewalk one fine afternoon. Two-way traffic is moving at the regulated maximum speed of 15 miles per hour. Then suddenly you hear a woman scream from across the street. You turn to look and spot an elderly woman in her seventies pleading for help as an assailant yanks her purse off her arm, pausing long enough to bury a hard kick to the ribs of the woman's unconscious husband who is laying on the sidewalk. The nearest crosswalk is a city block away in either direction. You were a combat medic in the Army for four years and you know you can help, that you need to help the old couple. What do you do?

If you follow the rules, you'll need to sprint up a city block, wait for the light to change, cross the street, and run back another city block to the distressed victims. Or you can dash across the street, ignoring the prohibition against jaywalking and administer lifesaving aid to the elderly man. Most people I know would ignore the rules in this case, risking traffic and a ticket for jaywalking. Even reading the first option sounds ludicrous; and I used this example to make my point, without the subtlety a legal process might entertain.

In life we rarely are confronted with such an easy ethical dilemma. More often they are complex and nuanced to the point of madness. I usually simplify all ethical challenges by first asking myself or my employees what the right thing to do is. Rules made by society, organizations, even families are not put in place having contemplated every possible scenario. We have minds and we need to use them when it comes to ethics.

Professional ethics are spelled out in codes of conduct. While many people are fired or prosecuted for ignoring these clear instructions, the ethical dilemmas we all face from time to time are rarely written down for us to reference. In these situations, we must take a deep breath, clear our minds, decide what is the right thing to do, and then act accordingly. Even if it means setting aside a rule for the moment. This is called using good judgment.

Morality

I won't get into the debate on morality between agnostics and atheists on one hand, and religious adherents on the other hand. For a person who believes in a religious doctrine, morality is clear and, like with professional codes of conduct, usually spelled out in a book or sacred tradition.

There are a lot of moral rules in the world's religions. They are embedded in sacred writing, formal teaching, and consistent in ceremonies. The very code of laws, English Common Law, that we as Americans use is based on a Judeo-Christian premise of moral conduct. Hundreds of years ago, there wasn't a separation between ethics and moral conduct; they were derived from the same source and inseparable. Over time, secularism during the Age of Enlightenment in Europe pitted logic and reason against a religious-based philosophy, and ethics and morality emerged as separate siblings in the practice of law.

Think of this comparison. The Bible says, "Thou shall not kill." All societies have laws against murder and see this as a higher, moral issue. "Thou shall not jaywalk," not so much. While the modern social debate over the question, "Can atheists have a moral code if they do not believe in God?" has moderated the definitions of morality and ethics (merging them as the same thing in recent dictionaries), so you can see from my comparison between murder and jaywalking that there is a practical distinction.

One classic example of ignoring morality is the practice of armed conflict between nations, and in the recent 60 years, between nations and non-state bad actors such as terrorists. I read a passage many years ago written by a psychologist trying to understand the effect the Vietnam War had on the returning veterans, even many years later. What struck me at the time, and why I still remember his words, was the simplicity of his observation. He explained that he'd concluded that a population of American youth, raised in a tradition of religious morality and Judeo-Christian law, were sent to the jungle thousands of miles away and ordered to ignore everything they'd been taught as children. Then, conversely, upon arriving home again, they were ordered to go back to the appropriate social norms of behavior.

Another writer commenting on war in general once stated that to a civilian at home, war is insane; and to a warrior in combat, civil rules and norms are insane. The implication being that we send sane people to war, and they learn to survive and come back, a reflection of that violent insanity. Affected in some cases so deeply, many veterans can never readjust to a sane worldview. I've never had to experience a sustained multi-year conflict, but I've had to ignore a few rules.

I was a 32-year-old Lieutenant Junior Grade, referred to as "JG," when I was tasked with recovering arms and, if possible, surrendering soldiers hiding in the commercial section of a large port. I was a former enlisted SEAL and had risen to Chief Petty Officer before gaining my commission and continuing as a SEAL leader. SEAL platoons of 16 fighters, referred to as "operators," were led by full Navy Lieutenants. Not in this case. I was given command of a SEAL platoon, despite the rules and due in large part to my prior senior enlisted knowledge, experience, and demonstrated judgment.

Even so, the mission was a tough one and they sent a more senior officer along just in case, a Lieutenant Commander. He was also a prior enlisted SEAL, having been a junior Petty Officer before heading out to Officer Candidate School in Newport, Rhode Island. We'd known each other since BUD/s training 13 years earlier. We flew out to a staging area and started working on a plan. I'd already led my platoon on 20 successful missions, and we were in the zone.

I asked the Lieutenant Commander how he wanted to do the job, and he just smiled. "It's your platoon, Marty. I'm just along for the ride. Just let me know how I can help." I was appreciative of this attitude. In my day, SEALs were free to operate without the technological oversight that exists today. We were more like pirate captains, set off to do the deed and get everyone back in one piece.

My team and I planned our action efficiently. We were happily surprised when we found an old, steel World War Two landing craft that was operational and used locally to ferry supplies around. We decided to use it as our floating castle for the trip into the port. The next morning, I checked in with my assigned helicopter gunships and found the Lieutenant Commander. He wasn't ready to go. As a courtesy, I'd briefed him the night before and just assumed he was coming with us.

The senior officer smiled at seeing the look on my face. "Marty, I told you before, this is your platoon. Your show. I appreciate you briefing me last night, but you and I know you are more than capable of doing this job. Truthfully, I'm only here because some of the other staff pukes got cold feet sending a JG here, even after your combat track record. So they sent me as insurance to cover their ass in case it goes south."

I shook my head. It made sense the rules had already been ignored by making a JG a SEAL platoon commander. I asked him about the communications plan. He stood up and placed a hand on my shoulder. He was ten years older, a former enlisted Marine before joining the Navy and becoming a SEAL. "I'll monitor the SATCOM and the other tactical nets. I'll be listening to the little birds watching over you, too. I don't plan to send the folks back at staff anything other than you have left and you are back. If they ask, I'll act like I'm having radio difficulty. Go get it done; I'll see you later."

With that, he gave my shoulder a pat and walked away. I smiled. I didn't intend to radio him either. Some rules can be ignored if by following them sound judgment is replaced with a risk-adverse committee trying to steer things from a hundred miles away. Understand, I was festooned with radio, signal flares, smoke grenades, and so were several of my men, not to mention the communications suite in the landing craft. If I needed anything at all, heaven and earth would be moved to accommodate my needs.

We captured 60 or so enemy soldiers, tossed a hundred weapons into the water, and took the packed landing craft back to our temporary base camp. I'll never forget the Lieutenant Commander's faith in me and his willingness to ignore the rules. We were shot at on the way in, while we were there sorting out prisoners and weapons, and all the time I was comfortable making each tactical adjustment as required. He was right: I was up to the task, and more.

Entrepreneurial Audacity

I met an interesting business owner a few years ago and was intrigued by his story. Now mind you, it was getting harder and harder to surprise or wow me with a never-before-seen business idea or unique method of business execution. My clients at UBS were mostly entrepreneurs, self-made millionaires many times over, and they were all mavericks. In this case as I sat there finishing the introductions, I couldn't help noticing the man was fatigued. Either because of sleep deprivation or physical exertion, he looked spent. That is until he began to speak to me about his company.

In the spirit of discretion, I'll call him Sam and his company Ajax, Inc. Sam was about 33, tall, probably an athlete once upon a time. He began telling me about his baby, Ajax Inc., and how he was disrupting everything. "That's right," he said, "everything." Not the baby formula industry or the fractional jet use industry, he said. "Everything," and I repeated the word. He looked at me and smiled. The fatigue that was so evident initially seemed to melt away. "Yes, everything!"

"Okay," I said. "Explain how you're doing that." He nodded and dove right in. I sat there listening for an hour, asking few questions. Apparently, Sam wasn't a specialist in the business he'd started, far from it. He was a construction guy. He'd spent many years after college working his way up the industry in Alabama, first as a foreman, then a project supervisor, and, eventually, as a senior manager of multiple building projects.

Sam, it seemed, had a skill that was critical in the construction world. He was able to select great subcontractors, keep them happy and on schedule, and deliver projects done right with time to spare. This knack, talent, special power was the reason for Sam's steady rise in the industry. Then one day a family member had a problem getting their lab results back in time for a key medical decision. Sam went to war; and as he untied the knot of confusion and ineptitude, he found his calling. Ajax, Inc. was born!

Sam began knocking on doors, offering lab services to whoever would speak with him. He was on a personal mission to improve the entire chain of activity associated with lab testing and lab specimen transport. What Sam now knew was that the market and the industry were steeped in traditions and processes that hadn't changed in decades. The speed of pickup and delivery was not driven by the customer/patient needs; it was what it was. Lab services operated like the DMV.

Sam wasn't getting the traction he needed knocking on doors. It seemed his promise to speed lab service up was disbelieved by the facilities he pitched. Eventually, he decided to ignore the rules of sales and marketing, too. Sam walked in and asked prospects, "What's keeping you up at night?" Whatever their answer was, Sam laid out a plan to solve their problem. He established medical billing units to solve poor billing issues and audiology units to improve that service. Eventually, once he was the solutions guy, he'd ask about lab services.

Sam also changed the supply chain equation. He recruited independent drivers to move the collected lab specimens to the labs. They operated like Uber or Lyft, hungry to execute at speed and as frequently as Sam needed them to. Sam soon had leverage based on the number of medical facilities he called clients. He confronted the labs themselves, providing a referral and fee to incentivize their speedy and accurate completion of lab analysis. Soon he used this as leverage to convince more facilities to use his services.

When I spoke with Sam, he'd busted out of Alabama and was operating and scaling in three states. Today his company is all over the eastern United States. Sam could have entered the market following the tried and true playbook, as defined and dictated by tradition, both in business planning, sales and marketing, and lab services; but he chose to ignore the traditions and instead be different.

Chapter Eleven

How to Make the Rules and Why

Any fool can make a rule, and any fool will mind it.
Henry David Thoreau

When I was a young Navy SEAL, I was trained in Arctic warfare. First in Canada, and then in Norway, three hundred miles north of the Arctic Circle. The mountains were ridiculously steep and difficult to climb wearing cross-country skis. We'd place wax on the bottoms of our skis to increase friction against the snow; but it wasn't enough, considering the dramatic terrain.

The Norwegians we worked with had a technique we used to good effect. One man would stab his ski pole tips into the hard snow behind the ends of the skis in front of him, and so on up the long line of commandos. This clever trick prevented the person in front of you from sliding backwards on the nearly vertical slope. We climbed, shuffling our skis forward a few feet, stabbing the pole tips into the snow, and waited for the next move. We repeated this for hours and hours each day as we ascended the bitter, cold mountains.

When I think of making rules, I reflect on this personal experience. The rules should be of value, but not sacred and forever locked in place. Human organizations of all sizes and shapes love to make rules, but hate to remove them. The result is an ever-increasing pile of restrictions and guidance, much of it stale, musty, and irrelevant. I like to think of rules like those ski pole tips. Valuable, effective, and then gone, having moved on to the next piece of terrain.

Rules should be impactful and constructed based on the context of the present and the future. Create them, use them, then discard them to make room for new ones. Shuffle, stab, shuffle, stab, and so on. Now, I can hear you saying to yourself, "Wait a minute! This guy hates rules! He's been bashing rules for the better part of twenty thousand words so far. So now he's embracing rules?" Well, yes, I am and here's why.

Standard Operating Procedures

SEALs and other special operators love their standard operating procedures or SOPs. Tactical reactions in combat are almost always an execution of a practiced SOP. They bind everyone together; they form the foundation of leader inspired actions. They keep an organization poised to react in a positive way to crisis or opportunity. Think of an SOP as a prearranged drill or list of actions that everyone understands and practices regularly. SOPs are rules for sure, but they are more than that. They are the core operating system of an organization or team.

Firefighters, emergency room technicians, power plant engineers, they all have well-rehearsed SOPs. A list of loosely associated rules, regulations, and norms isn't the same thing. If you have an active shooter policy, a fire drill policy, or a policy covering an employee in physical or mental crisis, and you have to have a meeting to figure out what to do next, then you don't have SOPs.

In the SEALs, SOPs are contextual. The tactical reactions in the desert differ from those in the mountains. A two-man reconnaissance mission may have different SOPs than a unit tasked with taking down a hotel as part of a hostage situation. Different aircraft require different SOPs. While the concept is simple, the number of SOPs can pile up. My approach to SOPS and rules is the same. SOPs can become stale, outdated, or inappropriate. In a transition period from jungle fighter to assault commandos, the SEALs had to scrap many beloved tactical formations and ways to communicate and plan in favor of what was required on a large complex urban target.

SOPs, like all effective rules, should be simple. The golden rule is an example. No fuss, no wordiness, effective and clear. A SEAL SOP that passes the simplicity test is the swim buddy rule. SEAL will do anything anywhere, but the lowest unit formation must be a two-man team. Swim buddies are based on another specific application from World War Two: nobody should swim alone. The word standard when used in this manner is less a quality value and more about standardization across many people or groups. Think about developing SOPs for your organization.

A Cradle of Creativity

Developing structure isn't the same thing as pursuing stability as an objective. Establishing guidelines, standards, customs, goals, and other structural elements is how we contain the possibilities long enough to lurch forward in a new and exciting way. Then we take a look around, modify, adjust, eliminate, or adopt new structural elements to lock in our hard-fought gains and reinforce a foundation that prepares us for the next leap forward.

Notice I'm not saying to establish traditions and rules that are sacred and unchanging. We are not looking for a new period of hardened arteries and closed minds. We are digging in, preparing for contingencies brought on by our audacious momentum, and then preparing for creativity to supercharge us into the future again and again. Leaders and smart followers should embrace this process—what the military refers to as a battle rhythm. Fight, win, clean weapons and equipment, eat, sleep, train, fight, repeat.

The innovation, inspiration, and invention that springs forth from creativity is awesome and yet fragile. We need to be attuned to this fact. One single person with great ideas is like a candle burning brightly in the darkness. It only illuminates a small circle of the room, and it only takes a slight movement of air to snuff it out. Leaders should strive to gather the candles together, to ignite more of them every day.

They should construct an environment where each bright light is safe from random or directed threats. They should aim to nurture this creative energy until it becomes a roaring fire of conviction and intent. Make the room bright; make your organization shine.

Of course, we've all witnessed the efforts by one leader or by management using policy to squelch, subdue, or extinguish creative input. The very fact that this is the normal condition is why I was compelled to write *Be Different*. Sure, promotions are nice, but they take us farther and farther away from the ground level activity. We rise to a place where the daily examples of negativism and pressure to conform and stop thinking are not as easy to see or experience personally. This deadens our senses, shields us from reality, and makes us a part of the problem. Don't be part of the problem!

Creativity Needs a Place to Thrive

So, when should you feel comfortable making rules? I suggest you perform the earlier exercise I described by evaluating the rules that are in place for a practicality and sanity check first. Often, new leaders arrive and immediately unpack a bag of new rules, ignoring the possibility that they are duplicating or confusing the intent of existing ones. Once you've finished, contemplate the who, what, when, where, why, and how of making a new rule.

First, should all rules be universal? Aligning guidance with surgical precision and detail will avoid the impression that the rule applies to all things, everybody, and everywhere. Also, in my experience, it is easier to craft, edit, or eliminate a finite rule than it is to do the same things with a decree covering a broad scope. Second, does the new rule make sense applied in every situation? At all times? Does it make sense in Albuquerque, New Mexico, and in Mumbai, India.

Making rules is serious business for all the reasons I've covered on the subject and many I have not. In government, it seems that once a rule is created, it can never die, regardless of how insane or odd it is. This lazy application of layered controls and direction are a boon to the legal firms brought in repeatedly to untangle years, even decades, of thoughtless, overlapping, and conflicting rules. So, when you sit down to make a rule, keep all this in mind and be smart, be clear, and above all, ensure that a rule is truly needed. Then keep it tight, contextual, and stay specific.

An environment without rules is as detrimental to creativity and innovation as an environment overwhelmed by restrictive edicts. The first situation allows for free thought, experimentation, and perhaps mindless abandon. Without guardrails, all this energy may be joylessly expended, but to no purpose. Inspiration that never sees development, projects held to no standard, and incredible insights with no timeline for implementation.

We've already discussed how an environment overburdened with regulatory weight crushes the creative spirit. So, we know that's to be avoided at all costs. What we need to constructively harness the energy and brilliance generated from thinking differently is a balanced approach. What we need is an environment safe enough to allow creative people and their thoughts to thrive safely, while at the same time imposing a discipline that eases that output into a process of practical design, development, and build. Creativity without application is a daydream, unfulfilled.

Baghdad, Iraq

For seven months I worked on a contract that provided high-end security services to the US State Department in Iraq. My initial reason for being in Iraq was commercial. I was scouting various business opportunities for a company in the United States and meeting with US and European technology groups to forge alliances and contracts. The insurgency was just beginning, and Iraq soon went from being a pacified environment of commercial opportunity to one of ambushes, improvised bombs, and chaos. I was asked to detach from my project, evaluate the state of security in general, and then specifically the state of mobile security protecting the US Ambassador and other senior US government officials.

At the time I'd been retired from military service for about nine years. However, I understood terrorism and security, so I agreed to help. What began as a 30-day commitment to consult ended up as a grueling seven-month experience leading 27 security teams and a small air force. When I walked into the large tent on the first day, I met 60 military veterans, all volunteers who were under contract to the State Department to act as protective officers. I asked them questions, trying to get a feel for what was going on. They didn't have any answers. For several weeks they'd been ignored and kept in the dark about their role and responsibilities. I soon determined it was because there were no leaders, not one.

It was hard for me to believe at first. Then I realized there also was no organizational structure in place. Every day, anywhere from five to 15 more men arrived, joining the original 60 I had met. I spoke with the State Department representatives, and they concluded the contract for protective services didn't include leadership positions or a structure for executing tasks. It was simply a staffing contract requiring former military professionals. That night I pulled everyone into a tent and began to speak. I wasn't sure how to fix the mess, but I was going to ask every one of those men to help me. I listened to their thoughts for an hour then had an idea. I asked them to reconvene the next evening with the biggest whiteboard they could find. We were going to invent our own organization.

The next night, the tent was packed with over 70 guys. I warned them it was going to be a nonstop marathon planning and design session; bathroom breaks were on them. We weren't going to stop until we were done. Nobody raised a stink, so I started. It was around six in the evening when we began and four in the morning when we finished. Nobody quit, nobody argued. It was a professional assessment in real time of every aspect of organizational design. We had three main operating groups and a fourth headquarters group. We had special teams, too. One for training new guys coming in from the states, one for intelligence planning, one for mission planning, one for managing the bomb sniffing detection dogs and their handlers, and one for scouting locations before the VIPs arrived.

By the time the sun came up, we had an organization, leadership positions, and a rudimentary ten-day training plan for new arrivals. Three days later, I briefed the State Department and they approved. That was the easy part. As it turned out, we needed rules. Rules for almost every conceivable situation. As we grew from 60 or 70 to 700 men, the rules became more and more critical to maintaining management control. I implemented a process that required all new rules to be submitted on no more than one typed page. Every night my top leaders and I would review the day's missions and challenges, and then examine the pile of rules suggested by the men in the organization.

I had stressed that the rules had to be fair, just, and simple to understand. We didn't have time to create a court. They had to be clear enough to avoid confusion by anybody. This was my leadership team's responsibility as they reviewed piles of ideas every night, seven days a week, week after week, month after month. To my pleasant surprise, it worked! As we expanded teams across Iraq, we copied the rules and placed them in three-ring binders. New approved rules or amended rules were sent by e-mail to the various sites, and they updated their book. Two years later when visiting for another purpose, I spoke with the man in charge of the protective service organization. Nothing had changed. The structure was intact. He proudly showed me a line of five three-ring binders filled with one-page rules. I was dumbfounded.

In the absence of rules, people need guidance and direction. Making rules is a serious undertaking, and I was humbled by the responsibility while I was in Iraq. Since that episode of my life, I've come to understand the value of rules and the value of revisiting the logic behind each rule periodically. Rules serve the leaders and the organization until the day they do not. Rules should not be open to frivolous criticism, but they should be soberly evaluated on a regular basis. Hand-in-hand with this is an evaluation of any penalties and punishments for not following the rules. As time passes, the original context that justified the rule or the punishment shifts, requiring mature review.

Making rules is important business. I suggest you start with as few as possible and let experience be your guide. In my Baghdad example, we didn't start out by trying to duplicate all the rules of the military or the State Department. We began simple, then worked our way to more complicated scenarios requiring more nuance. In a business or new organization, this works as well. If you are tasked with reviewing an existing pile of rules, consider keeping it simple, easy to understand, and relevant to the context of *now*. Fewer is always better. People are naturally willing to be pleasant, hard-working, and attentive to the tasks they are assigned. Assume this first, then grudgingly add rules to make it so. Avoid making a rule that applies to one bad apple's bad behavior. Deal with that person specifically; don't create or modify a rule in response. When it seems the rules are really confusing, trash them all and start clean.

Chapter Twelve

Architect of Change

There are risks and costs to action. But they are far less than the long range risks of comfortable inaction.
John F. Kennedy

Let's reflect on a few key points raised in the early chapters of this book before we move on to look at how we can construct an environment that is conducive to exploration, experimentation, and free intelligent thought. The human mind is designed to think both minutely and broadly. Both in terms of short-range context and long-range context. I am able to stay freely in the moment, zoom into the past, or jump forward into the future. The mind is capable of task focusing on a single outcome, and it can roam afar in search of new opportunities. In a nutshell, our brain is an awesome thing to behold.

Now for the impediments to full utilization of this wonderous organ. People are pressured at a young age to get serious, stop dreaming, and be constructive. We are conditioned during our formative years by learning institutions that praise rote memorization, compliance with historical practices, and adherence to norms. Social and cultural restrictions also impact the way we develop, with social objections to being different and thinking differently. Then we enter the workforce. More rules, more obedience, a doubling down on what is serious.

There it is. The yin and the yang of it. The awesome inspiring potential of the human mind versus a world full of practical, closed-minded risk managers. How should we begin? This book is about you and how you think or, more to the point, how you are naturally designed to think. So, I believe it is prudent to begin here, with you as an individual. Before you can become an architect of change, you must change. The following are five key elements of making that change.

Ways to Think Differently

Self-inventory is an approach I suggest in all my books. In the case of creativity, I ask that you first identify the obstacles preventing you from being more expressive and impactful. I've explained how our baggage, both personal and that imposed on us in the workplace, inhibits freedom of thought and therefore freedom of intellectual engagement. Take out a piece of paper or light up your preferred computing device and start listing these psychological impediments now.

Once you have your list, clean it up so it reflects three categories: people, place, and personal. The first two categories are things you may have to avoid or manage better. The third category is a bit tougher. You are the vessel that contains or exhibits the feelings, emotions, actions, and reactions that combine to define your creative strengths or weaknesses. While avoiding or managing threats and obstacles isn't easy, controlling yourself will be the most difficult task.

Self-discipline is the key to personal change and creative enlightenment. This is counterintuitive. Self-discipline is perceived by most of us as a means of control and restrictive behavior. Isn't this the opposite of intellectual freedom? Well, no, not really. A yogi practices mind-bending meditative states to become entirely free of intellectual and psychological constraints. An artist may allow their mind to fly free to find their muse while still behaving in a disciplined manner. Your path will be similar.

Self-discipline is all about establishing a pattern or habit that allows you to mentally and physically engage in a manner of your choosing. It protects you from reactive living and thinking. It protects your right to exercise your intellectual strengths in a focused or unfocused way, as you see fit. To reject the baggage and dismiss the obstacles to creative thought requires such discipline.

Self-awareness is the art of understanding where you are in the moment as well as in the bigger picture. Navy SEALs practice what they refer to as situational awareness. This is the practice of knowing the context of your current situation. In a combat environment, this becomes a critical survival skill. In life or at work, a similar criticality exists. Who wants to stumble blindly into a bad outcome?

Poise is a form of self-awareness. Being calm while under fire means you are intensely aware of your circumstances, but not distracted or overwhelmed by those circumstances. Clearing your mind to absorb and evaluate your surroundings, including both your physical environment and the human activity directly or indirectly interacting with you, is the foundation of self-awareness. Once achieved, this foundation allows you to apply your mind to the possibilities, the contingencies, the greyness, or the brightness of your world.

Self-esteem is how you see yourself. Unfortunately, we are usually too worried about how others see us, and as a result we question our own value. To grow and evolve, we must be honest with ourselves and use the context of the world we live in to make sure that assessment is logical. What is not logical is absorbing and accepting assessments made by other people about you as truth. It is not truth. It is untested, unquestioned, and, in some cases, insight delivered to you based on envy, anger, fear, or many other base motivations.

Knowing ourselves is how we shred the baggage others have packed into our minds. Imagine an attic packed to the rafters with boxes and boxes of old memories, junk, and miscellaneous items we can't bring ourselves to discard. Now picture the attic cleared of that mess. You can see all the way to the end of the attic; you have clarity. Self-esteem is what we give ourselves, what we create for ourselves, not the accumulation of other people's opinions.

Selflessness is one way to become willing to accept insight, information, and eventually change. You don't have to be Mother Teresa or Mahatma Gandhi selfless. That bar is far too high. You only need to be open to different. Different triggers all the baggage, it stimulates instinctive counter-reactions based on years of psychological and emotional conditioning. Different is a threat unless you see it as an opportunity. Set aside your urge to think in your own interests to the exclusion of other possibilities. Selflessly accept different and see what happens.

Another side effect of selflessness is an awakening of purpose. A purpose greater than your to-do list, greater than your personal goals. Selfless behavior means walking the earth looking for ways to assist, help, and intercede to the benefit of others, not just yourself. Take this point of view into the workplace and imagine how much good you can do as a mentor, coach, guide, or just another pair of helping hands. Not for recognition, a raise, or a promotion … just because. Can you envision what the world and your organization would look like, feel like, if everybody conducted themselves in this way?

Handling Blowback

I write about this challenge in my book *Be Visionary*. Being a change agent isn't for the faint of heart. People will not universally grasp the import or the value in the beginning; some will never understand. This, alas, is normal. People are people, and they have different points of view. Most would not be willing to evolve and adopt the five attributes or behaviors we've just discussed. That is why it is so important that you do adopt them. You need to be prepared for the emotional onslaught, the negativism, the undermining, and the social shunning created by your initiative. You need to be ready for the blowback.

Blowback is a commonly used term used to describe the totality of consequences associated with an action. Figuratively, it attempts to give the impression of a counterwave of sentiment, contrary behavior, and damage caused by an action. I was years into experiencing this before someone coined the phrase, but the meaning is spot on. In 1991, the United States Special Operations Command, or SOCOM, began to flex its muscles. The command was created by Congress to gather up all the special units across the Army, Navy, and Air Force and place them under one roof. This law was enacted in the mid-1980s; but in 1991, the new rules began to rain down from the new organization.

I was working in the Naval Special Warfare Center's Strategy and Tactics Group, located in Coronado, California, only a few blocks away from the offices of our SEAL admiral and his staff. One day I was summoned to accompany my commanding officer for a meeting with the admiral. The topic was bizarre, unfathomable, and official. SOCOM at the time was comprised of nearly all career Army officers, from the four-star general at the top all the way down. Many were suspicious of the other services' special operations skills, but now that was about to be corrected.

My captain and I entered the admiral's office and were directed to sit down. We were each handed a single white piece of paper and told to read. The admiral sat back and waited. I read the document three times before I spoke up. I was a combat-experienced SEAL officer; my captain was a bona fide Vietnam hero in the Teams. Each of us wore the same dumfounded expression. The new four-star general in charge of all US special operations was ordering all SEALs, every SEAL, regardless of position, experience, or age, to attend and pass the US Army's rigorous Ranger School course.

"Thoughts, gentlemen?" The admiral's face was serious, grave even. I said what popped into my mind. "Is this a way of telling us we aren't tough enough to be in SOCOM?" The admiral nodded and glanced at his chief of staff. "That's exactly what it is. My counterpart in Air Force Special operations also received the same order. Every member of every aircrew, every pilot, every combat control, and para rescue professional. I spoke to him a few minutes ago."

My captain was a big guy. A former NCAA wrestling star and nationally recognized power lifter *before* leading SEALs in Vietnam. I could see he was about to blow his top and so did the admiral, raising his hand to fend off the tirade we all knew was coming. We knew it was a mistake, ill-informed, and potentially catastrophic for us and our Air Force partners. We were told to go back to our command and produce a plan. My captain regained his composure and said, "Marty and I can work on that on our way to Fort Benning, Georgia."

We were on a plane that afternoon, a Friday, headed to the home of US Army Ranger School. When we arrived, we set up a meeting for the next morning with the commanding officer of Ranger School. That meeting was eye opening and informative. The Army had determined that Ranger School wasn't only a test of stamina and grit. It also had concluded it was more valuable as a way to harden and prepare leaders for the rigors of combat. For a few years before the arrival of the order for SEALs to attend, the Army had radically increased the influx of students to achieve this secondary objective.

Simply put, the senior Army officers at SOCOM wanted to see a Ranger badge, referred to as a "Tab," on the shoulder of every member of SOCOM, regardless of parent service. More as a guarantee of leadership confidence than a certification of toughness. Still, we had a huge problem. Ranger School was overwhelmed. They didn't have the room or the instructors to add even one hundred more students a year, not without pushing aside Army candidates, and we all knew that wasn't going to happen.

So my captain, the Ranger School commanding officer, his senior enlisted advisor, and I spent hours cooking up a strategy to make it all go away. Our eventual solution was a challenge to the egos of those in power at SOCOM. Out tough, out lead, out soldier the Army on hallowed ground. We created a second version of Ranger School that was more difficult in key areas.

This Special Operations Light Leader Course would be staffed by SEALs, Air Force commandos, and Ranger instructors. To make it work, we needed to fly to Florida and sell it to the Air Force. Twenty-four hours and a lot of beer and Jack Daniels later, the Air Force was a go. Now we had to convince our admiral to buy into the plan. A key component of this approach was to execute the course only once, but in such a way that demonstrated once and for all that SEALs and Air Force warriors were elite professionals and that Ranger School wasn't required.

The admiral gave us the green light, and this is where the concept of blowback comes in. Not from SOCOM, but from our fellow SEALs. My mission was to brief all the commanding officers of all the SEAL Teams on the plan and then get a list of high-speed super SEALs from each. These apex SEALs, plus the more difficult course events, would end the nightmare forever.

The admiral's staff informed the SEAL Team captains that I was on my way to brief them regarding a sensitive project. I started the circuit telling the story, highlighting the threat, namely the disruption of every training and deployment cycle at every SEAL Team and the loss of twenty to twenty-five percent of the operator population as they attended the Ranger course. Despite the admiral's endorsement, the chief of staff's directives, and my best efforts, my briefings were largely ignored.

You see, I was a lowly lieutenant at the time and the leaders of each separate SEAL Team were Navy commanders. Their reactions stunned me. They were angry they were not part of planning and they were dismissive of the threat, calling it a figment of the admiral's imagination. They were in a state of disbelief regarding SOCOM's premise that SEALs were not tough or good leaders. Only a handful even heard me out, and not one was willing to give me the names of their uber SEALs for the project.

When I'd completed my task, I went back to my captain having failed to accomplish anything except making a handful of senior SEALs dislike and distrust the messenger ... me. What happened next was worse. The admiral sent a personal message ordering compliance with my request. Again, rather than see the threat and the logic of our plan, the recipients of that order negatively tagged my name to the project. Yet, the Teams sent their best SEAL operators, and two months later we started the initial course at Fort Benning, Georgia. I was there to oversee the event.

Now here's the point of this story about blowback. The crazy idea we came up on a Saturday morning worked! By the time half the course was completed, the Army brass at Fort Benning, and even the retired generals living around the base, were burning up the phones at SOCOM. The elite SEALs and Air Force commandos were embarrassing the Army on hallowed ground. A few weeks later, the course ended forever; and the drive to force SEALs and other special operators through Ranger school died with it.

I received two medals for this project. One from the admiral and one from the colonel who ran the Ranger school program. As for the SEAL community? It was assumed I was the sole reason the various commanding officers were rebuked. Not because they failed to grasp the enormity of the threat, but because I was a busybody trying to score points at the expense of others. I knew better and so did the admiral and my captain, who became the next SEAL admiral and spoke at my retirement ceremony. To this day SEALs from that era stare blankly when

I tell them how close we all came to disaster. Nobody knew, nobody cared, but we stopped the threat just the same.

Is the Juice Worth the Squeeze?

My answer to this question is a resounding yes! If your mind and heart are in the right place and the change you create is impactful in a positive way, then absolutely, yes! Being the architect of change is a lonely place to be, that is if you do it all by yourself. In my blowback example, I had allies, but suffered through the day-to-day execution of the plan alone. I have many other examples in the military and in business, where the stakes were high and the need to act decisively and creatively were obvious and compelling. It is always more difficult if they are not.

In the case of the Ranger school story, we failed to communicate the challenge and the consequences appropriately. In other words, by sending a junior officer, the message was perceived as less important. I suggest you try spending as much time on the communications plan as you do on the solution to your challenges. Even the best designs need to be pitched well before resources are applied and construction of the new normal begins.

Have a bias for action, thoughtful action to be sure, but action, nonetheless. Pondering and musing sounds cool, but even the most courageous and incredible ideas and insights need to exit one's head to be valuable. Risk blowback, ridicule, even risk social consequences. If you dare to be different, then you will be different and therefore will reap what you sow. Maybe not immediately; but someday, when the positive changes and initiatives you conceived, designed, and delivered are a part of the history of your organization. Dare to dream, dare to act, dare to be different!

Chapter Thirteen

Engineering Change

You can't go back and change the beginning, but you can start where you are and change the ending.
C.S. Lewis

This book is about creative energy; more importantly, it's about why it's okay to release that creative energy. A scholarly friend of mine, Michael Steiner, Executive Director of BEST Robotics, Inc., read one of my articles and shared his takeaways with me. He'd recently attended a multi-day national conference on creativity. He explained that there were disagreements, academic differences of opinion on the definition of creativity and innovation.

Michael is a former senior Israeli military officer who came to the United States and eventually gained citizenship. He was widely known as an architect of organizational and policy change in Europe before settling into a post at Carnegie Mellon University. There he was tasked with developing a for-profit extension of the university, establishing training and educational courses for corporations and global governments. He went on to work in the field of competitive robotics as a business mentor and strategist.

As I listened to my friend, he explained to me that on one hand, a case was being made that creativity was, by itself, an expression of innovation. But on the other hand, some attendees at the conference felt that creativity was a first step toward progress, and innovation was the second logical step or outcome of that creative flow. As we chatted about this debate, Michael cited something I'd written and noted; while he'd been on the fence listening to the discourse at the creativity conference, he had a flash of insight related to my writing on the subject.

Michael reflected that the terms *creativity* and *innovation* could be assumed to be similar in intent. However, he remembered that I've made a habit of making a case in my musings that to *be* creative is different, and different is valuable. He went on to say that he believed I was correct. That there wasn't a significant conflict between *being* creative and *being* innovative. They were both essentially the same expression of intellectual inspiration.

I saw his point, but wasn't sure I'd actually made that detail in my work. In fact, this was a fusion of my themes and Michael's brilliance. He added one last point. If these two terms are the expression of intellect, then they are twins, both the fountainhead of change. That means they do not conspire to build a two-step process, but are actually a unique way to describe or label the first step in the process of change. He ended our call with the following insight. The second step is implementation. Implementation is the engineering of inspiring intellectual thought. The second step in the flow. It's how things change. We build.

Study the Blueprints

As an author of both fiction and nonfiction, I'm accustomed to the process of rewriting. This is a complex activity that is more involved than simply using the spelling autocorrect feature on your computer. It involves humility and honesty. As the creator, you are in love with your creation. You poured your heart and soul into the first draft and can't bring yourself to mess with perfection. Perfection? Well, perhaps not perfect, but nearly perfect. To make it better requires stamina, an open mind, allies, and courage. Humility helps, too.

The same holds true with any creative draft. You or a team of developers may have solved the challenge or designed the next big thing, but it won't be perfect, at least not yet. A rule of thumb often repeated among creatives is to set the work aside for a while. Let it breathe. Which really means let your mind disengage and reset for a period before picking the project back up for a fresh look. This same approach is appropriate for all creative designs. The architect of change creates the outline, or a more detailed vision of their innovative design, and then lets it season a bit. Trust me, I've come back to my work after a hiatus and spotted glaring discrepancies in logic, silly notions half-formed, and worse. It takes humility and patience to build the future.

Enlist Allies

I sent every chapter of all 11 of my books to beta readers as they were created. A beta reader is a trusted ally who has the wisdom and experience to evaluate your creative work and provide constructive feedback. Derived from the concept of "beta testing" innovative ideas in manufacturing and technology, this third-party honest appraisal technique is invaluable. I suggest you enlist other creatives to help you in the early design process as well. Most ideas spring from a sloppy collision of inputs, arguments, and misunderstandings. Once the "aha!" moment happens, you arrive at an idea, but do not have a fulsome concept of how to bring the idea to life. When I write my books, I look for a few people interested in the genre the book represents. They possess experience reading similar work and act as a stand-in for my intended audience. In other endeavors, you might seek end users, integrators, resource decision makers, and so on. The point is to expose the creative blueprint to the objective criticism of those who will interact with or buy your idea once it comes to life. I've used this method countless times in business, and it works. The rapid prototyping of your concept into a workable, functioning result can be frustrating and at the same time exhilarating.

Secure Resources

I speak about this topic in my book *Be Visionary*. In most organizations, there are processes established that inform us how to request additional resources for a current project or a new resource commitment for a new project. You should become familiar with these opportunities if you wish to constructively implement your creative and innovative ideas. The simple sequence for an enlightened thinker who wants to make a difference looks like this: idea to concept, concept to blueprint, resource support, development, testing, implementation, and measure. Securing resources for your idea is a critical requirement.

Competition among priorities for the allocation of internal resources is a never-ending struggle. Old themes, stale budgets rolled forward without thought, other ideas searching for approval, and of course the demand of day-to-day business operations. I've learned a few tricks over the years that may be helpful to you. First, become fluent in the resource request process. Second, consider breaking your project into baby steps to reduce the cost per activity allowing you natural pause points as things progress. Third, devise a pilot or beta test as proof your concept works. This last thought secures startup funding and support, and demonstrates the value of your creative idea before greater organizational resources are committed.

Expect Resistance

Like blowback, resistance is a natural consequence of being different. Resistance can manifest in many ways and originate in the strangest places. Friends and colleagues may subtly derail your success for your own good. Management personalities might be envious of your creative aura or fearful that you'll rock the boat and get them in trouble. Other departments or divisions may be working on the same challenge but failing, and you are a threat to their credibility.

When you experience resistance, try to see it as a positive sign; you're stimulating discussion and consideration of alternative thinking. You may gain allies and converts when generating intellectual unrest, but you will most assuredly gain naysayers, saboteurs, and serious opposition. It goes with the territory; and as I've harped on for quite some time, change and the leaders of change will always spark passionate and emotional opposition. The trick is to not allow this natural counterflow to inhibit or douse your creative spirit.

I'll share a story with you to illustrate how resistance can appear and evolve. Several years ago, our company was about to sign a teaming agreement with a large defense firm to provide the Navy with an online learning product. One of my executives walked into my office and said he was going to kill the agreement because we didn't have experience creating online or virtual learning products. The big defense firm wanted us because of our deep relationship with the Navy customer, but that was the only value add. I sat back and began to think.

The result of that conversation was frantic open-source research, while in parallel we sought freelance experts in online and virtual learning platforms. We had a lot of knowledge related to training development, so I set up another team to create a basic course that, once converted to a virtual learning experience, would serve as a demonstration of our capabilities. These three tracks ran simultaneously for a few days before I pulled everyone into a room for feedback.

What they'd gathered was telling. We had a new course outline, we had an instructional systems design expert, and we had a film production and graphics company identified. While everyone in my group complained and moaned about the foolish project, they'd actually demonstrated that we could make it happen. And so we did! We confidently signed the teaming agreement, developed, tested, and created the virtual learning product, and then briefed the Navy on our team's combined capabilities.

Sounds like a success story, right? Not so fast. The new and entirely unexpected source of resistance we encountered was the Navy. Our customer's internal training experts were retired Navy personnel whose average age was around 55. They wanted no part in our virtual learning capabilities and asked in the strongest terms for a simple video. We lobbied and explained to no avail. In the end we acquiesced and produced a video. Go figure!

Embrace Experimentation

In the early days of the NASA space program, experimentation was a normal process of trial and error, every single day. Experimentation involves risk taking, resource use, and yes, waste. It requires courage of conviction and a nimble mind. As time went on, the population working the various NASA programs got older and older and older. Risk taking was replaced with mistake avoidance. Those in authority who rose to the top through brave experimentation were now dedicated to stability at any cost.

Engineering innovative concepts isn't, I'll say it, rocket science, but then again it is. If you adopt the mindset of those early engineering pioneers and take big chances, then you will reap big rewards. Experimentation is how we all learned to walk, to talk, to ride a bike. In my opinion, the death of creative architecture relies heavily on the attitude, not the aptitude, of those who build the dream. If you can influence this phase of implementation, do so with risk taking not risk mitigation in mind.

The essence of experimentation is do, fail, learn, and try again. This holds true for the smallest and least impactful element, as well as the most significant and critical element of your design. In my experience, innovative programs start with exciting speeches, rousing kickoffs, and inspiring project names. Then, more often than not, the team works hard to conform to whatever they've built in the past. This default to a comfort zone is honest and very human. You should anticipate this reaction and engage regularly to ensure it doesn't happen. To walk away and trust is a recipe for disappointment.

You Must Lead

While the innovative designer may not be the actual engineer of change, they should stay close to the process. The idea-to-concept, concept-to-blueprint process establishes the goals, the outcomes, and the expectations. The designer is the expert on this process and the end state. Placing this person or persons in charge of the overall change project is a terrific way to prevent regressive thinking, and worse, regressive engineering. This is the prospect that the builders will undo the creativity and innovative features to "normalize" the build. Subtly turning strawberry ice cream into vanilla.

The leader doesn't have to be a senior executive. You can have regular project leadership titles and roles and have a creative director. I suggest this person report directly to the sponsor authority for the change project. This keeps everybody honest and attentive to the creative lead's input. Creative leads also must listen to the engineers. Building a high-rise involves gravity, which cannot be wished away in order to build a whimsical architectural vision.

The same goes with practicality. At some point, the ability to dream around corners will run into tangible challenges that cannot be solved. Cars need propulsion, planes need lift, glass is fragile, people need to stay safe, and a hundred other considerations. Once, while working on counterthreat assessments for the 2004 Olympics in Athens, Greece, the team focused on both safety and fun realized you cannot have one to the exclusion of the other. A perfect bulletproof, bombproof sphere addresses the threat and security challenges, but it defeats the Olympic attendee's freedom to move happily from one venue to another. Practicality and balance were required.

The Rapid Prototype Approach

I'm friends with quite a few inspiring entrepreneurs, and I learn something from them every time we engage. They reflect a wide range of industries and vocations, and this diversity is compelling to me as a creative thinker. Most are thoughtful and clever when in the design mode and aggressive when in the implementation mode. They are not Navy SEALs, but they are fearless, nonetheless. Most ascribe to the theory that perfection isn't an ideal you achieve, it's an ideal you pursue; and on the way to perfection, close is good enough. They are all leaders, all willing to experiment, and all willing to bench test their constructed concepts in the field, which includes buyer and end user sourcing of critical feedback.

Rapid prototyping is a wonderful way to shake the kinks out of your design; and in most cases, user experience data is the only reality check that matters. I'm not telling you I approve of applying this to passenger aircraft, prescription drugs, or any activity where not getting it right the first time holds dire consequences. I'm saying it's a viable method that accelerates feedback and redesign.

While I'm using words from the manufacturing and production lexicon, all the creativity hacks in this book apply to everything you want to change for the better. Human business processes, the arts, politics, governance, any area of human endeavor. The engineering world gave us the gift of linear planning and production, and it works in describing how to progress from idea to implementation. However, it is only a guideline. Use it, use a portion of the method, or don't. I'll be the last one to tell you there is only one way to breathe life into your creative work.

Watching the Magic Unfold

For me, the creative start is an awesome experience. Watching the idea being built is a close second. People who specialize in building things are artisans and deserve our respect. As I've noted, an idea without implementation is simply a daydream. Source your builders wisely. Strive to collect those who have expertise, but don't think like experts. These folks will see the wonder of your design and appreciate it, even the difference it represents. They won't fight you to reassert normal or ignore you by building blah, despite your design.

Managing implementation is critical to preventing accidental, subtle, and not so subtle, sabotage of your innovation. Fewer disconnects occur if you are paying attention throughout the build or implementation process. I once created a business plan based on someone else's creative idea. We'd bought the company and this fledgling vision. I worked hard to supersize the concepts and stood back after a few months, content with my creation.

My business plan was a perfect blend of practical and not so practical, at least from the point of view of the industry. I'd incorporated the seller's insights and ideas in a way we could execute. Growth was the name of the game, and the revamped company was ready. Then I handed the keys to a leader I trusted and respected. To this day he is an exceptional business executive working for a large defense firm. However, in this case, the implementation of my business plan, well, didn't go as planned.

There are distinctive styles of leadership and management, and one should endeavor to match up the right profile with the right challenge. I did not in this example. After a year, the company was operating like a fine Swiss watch. Every task, process, and system hummed along brilliantly. There was only one catch: we were barely growing, and growing was the strategic mandate. Great plan plus mismatched leader equals failure of the great plan.

Watching the magic is both a suggestion to have fun and a mandate to stay engaged. Don't simply become an idea machine, churning out creative thoughts and innovative blueprints for change that are run into the ground, normalized, or set aside completely by the ones tasked with building your masterpiece. I'm not telling you all engineering professionals are ready to trash your plan. I'm saying what I've noted through this book — people are people. Keep your creative eye on the ball and shepherd your project through to successful completion. Being different means being aware as well as insightful.

Chapter Fourteen

Artificial Intelligence

I am telling you, the world's first trillionaires are going to come from somebody who masters AI and all its derivatives and applies it in ways we never thought of.
Mark Cuban

The promise of AI speaks for itself. I know, cheesy, right? In searching for a poignant quote regarding the impact of artificial intelligence, I discovered the majority reflected near apocalyptic outcomes. Fears of a world dominated by a master race of AI-enabled robots, capable of perpetual regeneration through the magic of machine learning, abound in the media and with the public at large. Meanwhile, tech gurus scream AI's praise on every cable show, tweeting and posting, projecting a vision of benevolence and empowerment for humanity. What is the truth?

Bill Seith is a huge proponent of AI and its near limitless capacity to change our world for the better. Bill is a true renaissance man. An entrepreneur, general contractor, instructional systems design guru, uber smart marketing professional, and one of the most creative people I know. He also is a good friend and fellow Navy SEAL alumni. During a recent conversation, Bill asked how I was addressing AI in *Be Different*. I confessed I didn't have a single word dedicated to the subject. He went silent for a moment and then took me to school.

Using machine learning capabilities to create content is a simple definition of AI's generative design function. It transforms your input into an outcome that may be reflective of reality or a construct of a new reality. And here's the rub when it comes to creativity. Is AI a substitute source of innovation, or is it a supportive tool that enhances our natural ability to be creative? With every day that passes, I hear and read and learn more about this amazing capability. I would be silly to ignore the discussion and the debate regarding AI. Don't sit on the sidelines and wait; seek knowledge and catch up with this mega trend. It's better to understand and make sound decisions regarding AI's application than to get run over by the rapid evolution of this technology.

I'll confess up front that I'm, like most of you, learning about this technology as I go along. I have become comfortable enough to see practical applications in small ways. Our company is using it for marketing and promotion content development, formal business e-mails, and design of business proposals. It is applauded by the employees who don't have great skill and experience as writers. I place this AI-enabled activity firmly in the supporting tool category. However, as I dug deeper into the AI wave, I saw the root cause for people's concern.

We Are at the Starting Line

Artificial intelligence has been around for a long time. Attempts to program a thinking, evolutionary computer started in the early twentieth century at the very beginning of the computer age. As a kid there was a drumbeat of AI-themed science fiction thrillers. Smart robots, cyborgs, unmanned vehicles, super computers that became so smart they decided man was a nuisance, and so on. If you grew up with this negative narrative, you can't help but have *Terminator* PTSD. Is Skynet already here? Will machines rule the planet in the not too distant future? Yikes!

Of course, science fiction is just that, fiction. It may have a basis in fact or developing capabilities, but it is not prophetic. That is unless we become inspired by that fiction and embrace it as a worthy goal. This briefly describes the conflict over AI—a near visceral fear of a future, unknown but loosely defined by Hollywood, and a promise of nirvana. As with most things, the truth is somewhere in between, and we have the power and the responsibility to steer AI toward the light.

I've spent a considerable amount of time over the last five years listening to creatives and business professionals. My thoughts are formed as I roll, and my books reflect my understanding and insights at the time I wrote down those words. As far as AI, my learning curve began first with my association with the BEST Robotics, Inc. board of directors, then their extended technology brain trust, and finally by reading and asking dumb questions. It's the way I absorb things, and it seems to work. As I've traveled this path, a few salient thoughts kept popping up.

The Two-Pound Cell Phone

The Motorola DynaTAC 8000x hit the market in 1983, weighing in at a hair over two pounds! It took hours and hours to charge and lasted about 40 minutes. Around the same time, SEALs were issued a wide array of innovative technology related to communications and navigation. We were not fans for three reasons: the devices were always too big, too heavy, and unreliable.

In the mid-eighties, the SEALs were presented with an advanced, high-technology navigations system. We were trained to rely on charts, a good compass, and dead reckoning, a method of tracking progress across the water. We memorized coastal navigation aids, knew where the city lights ended by latitude and longitude, and so on. Boys following buoys. We were ordered one day to prepare a test of the new navigation system.

This new shiny toy didn't work off satellites; that capability was still half a decade away. This system worked off land-based radio signals. We were directed to parachute two combat rubber raiding craft, engines, fuel, eight SEALs, and the new toy from an Air Force C-130 cargo plane at night. Once in our boats at a point 30 nautical miles at sea (the visual horizon ends at 20 nautical miles, so we could not see America from our drop point in the Atlantic), we would aim for the mouth of the Chesapeake Bay using only the new navigation system. No compasses allowed.

What happened next is all about patience. Not during the mission, but patience regarding new technology, its initial promise, and the long development and learning curve associated with that technology. We got lost, really lost. Out of fuel floating off the state of North Carolina lost. To add insult to misery, the Coast Guard had to rescue us 14 hours later. The rescue took so long because nobody, neither our command nor the Coast Guard, had thought it possible we might decide to head for Savannah, Georgia. Having found nothing in the designated operational area, the search widened beyond the entrance to the Chesapeake Bay.

I can tell you stories for hours about crazy test and evaluation horror stories. Early satellite communications, satellite navigation, and yes even the first Motorola cellular phone. Since then, it hasn't really improved much, except I'm not ordered to buy a PalmPilot, a BlackBerry, or any of at least 20 variations of phones, computers, and smart phones over the last 20 years. What I learned was patience. I also learned respect for the evolutionary development curve across all types of technology. I believe AI will be no different.

A Replacement for Human Creativity?

I've learned from my friends in high technology that what the open-source AI people are interfacing with now is today's two-pound cell phone. I've also learned that the true design frontier is already generations beyond what we are allowed to see and play with for free. A massive amount of funding by the world's top militaries since the late 1990s was duplicated and ramped up by commercial corporations in the early 2000s seeking a competitive advantage. The AI race was on!

If the definition of AI is a generative, knowledge access knowledge-seeking software algorithm, my first question is who's feeding the beast? As we've seen with crowdsourced platforms like Wikipedia, input isn't filtered, vetted, or validated. It is just input, or worse, opinion pretending to be fact. As I write this chapter, a story came over the wire about a judge sanctioning two attorneys. Apparently, their AI written court brief contained useful but fictional legal citations. Are we back to garbage-in garbage-out? Will AI draw its wisdom from the same murky well of random inputs or just make things up?

I recently tested a commercial AI application and asked, "Who is Marty Strong?" At first the information was spot-on, based entirely on my social media and advertising materials. Then the data took a trip into fantasy Marty. It said I captured the first POW in the Iraq War; it attributed me a random smattering of combat awards, none of which was true. In essence, it decided I was a Navy SEAL, and once at the end of Marty information, it decided all Navy SEAL information was attributable to me.

One line of public and industry AI debate is the question of human creativity. Will AI outperform humans by speed of insight, quality of innovative inspiration, or the impact of its spectacular breakthroughs? Is it going to be about volume (AI can create 24/7/365; humans cannot), or the sheer ingenuity of AI in comparison to what we as humans can produce? If so, why complain? Wouldn't we benefit from this boon?

I guess the response to the value proposition argument depends on the category of development. Who needs hyper lethal and undetectable weapons systems? Wouldn't we rather have AI cure cancer? My concern is we will not be making a conscious and collective decision as human beings or even citizens to agree either way. It is all happening now, and it is accelerating into every corner of our world. Should we embrace this momentum or start buying survival kits?

At a minimum, a human created by deed or thought is the repository of information AI draws on to operate. As it combines, mixes, and analyzes the data, it will develop new data sets associated with that analysis. This too will become part of the reservoir within public or private AI domains. This means humans should continue to be creative, more creative than ever before. AI provides a thinking partner that can run alongside you, sprint ahead through analysis and modeling, and then fall back into position at your side. This is my vision of a positive application. A human creativity boom, enabled and empowered by AI, not crushed by it.

AI as Competition

Now I'm not speaking here of the sort of competition that pits us against evil AI-enabled robots. I'm speaking instead of parallel creative platforms. Human intellect, individually or collectively, and AI, each operating unilaterally and in coordination, without restrictions for restrictions' sake. What's the downside? On one hand, we keep doing what we've done forever: think, create ideas, execute. Meanwhile AI is doing the same, just differently.

I'm not sure restricting or channeling AI and human effort would be beneficial either, leaving we humans to focus on literature, music, and art (as intrinsically human endeavors) while AI focuses on disease, new energy sources, space exploration, and industrial efficiency. I prefer parallel efforts, across a wide range of challenges, and parallel progress, interactive and mutually empowered, not combative.

There is one area of concern that may be worth considering, and it is not only an AI issue. That is the issue of human employment. Again, the Armageddon crowd already have projected a robot utopian future with powerless human drones relegated to servicing the robot overlords. Might this happen? Maybe, if we collectively allow it to happen. I suggest this dire outlook is only half true.

Blue collar and knowledge-based work will be at risk in the coming decades as first programmed industrial robots are mass produced to invade every aspect of our world, and again as AI-enabled platforms take jobs from us. To understand how this might come to pass, you only need to study the history of automation. Automation affects every aspect of our industrial and personal life. Everything from harvesting corn to coffee makers and autonomous cars. These changes were both small and large, subtle and flamboyant. AI's march to prominence will be no different. If we see a different future, we have time to prepare for that future.

Automation wiped out jobs from the invention of the cotton gin in 1794 to the installation of food ordering kiosks at McDonalds in present-day America. Life has continued to thrive through all this historical change, but the most affected were those who stood still wishing for the change to go away. The people who learned how to win in the new normal adapted and moved forward. We should follow their example.

AI and Intellectual Property Protection

I'm careful not to take insights, theories, and quotes from other sources without specific attribution and credit. I refrain from reading books and articles related to the books I am writing, so I can focus on my thoughts and ideas in a clean and unambiguous manner. AI, however, sucks data in from everywhere and everybody. Once published or posted, the information is out there for the taking. Laws and rules protect intellectual property. Will AI care? Is all the poetry, music, art, and intelligence of humanity a free resource for

AI-enabled authors to exploit without attribution or risk of plagiarism?

A friend recently suggested I use AI to assist in my writing. I immediately reacted negatively. My thoughts and ideas, however insane, accurate, or confusing, are *my thoughts*. Why would I crowdsource a term paper in school and expect the grade to reflect my personal abilities? It would not. An artist doesn't paint by committee. AI is a boon for general writing projects, formatted work like business plans, newsletters, contracts, applications, and basic media prose. It allows people without the gift of narrative expression to cheat and complete their tasks on time and within expectations. I don't see the harm in this, and neither should you.

A master copy is still a copy. Examples of AI art are posted every day for us to admire. The styles, lighting, and subjects are all discoverable, their sources uniquely human. An AI *Mona Lisa* is still a copy of da Vinci's genius, not genius itself. It is in this specific area of intellectual property and source coding of AI production that I have an issue.

For example, we all know that Pablo Picasso is no longer with us, but let's say for a moment that he was still alive, and nobody knew of him. Then his first unique painting is discovered. Soon many of his works became well known. So different, so purely abstract. Up to this point, an AI platform would not have access to this form of artistic expression because it didn't exist in the database.

With AI's discovery of Picasso's first celebrated painting, this all changes. Now AI can replicate Picassos every minute of every day. The artist's spark of inventive insight and creative genius is turned into a commodity overnight. Sound farfetched? Actors are now being replicated by AI. The voices of regular people like you and me are being copied, too. An example of a scam sweeping the country right now looks like this. A family member calls home asking for money, convincing mom to help her child out of a financial dilemma. Except it isn't a daughter or son making the call. It's an AI program that's mimicked their voice perfectly. Be on guard and be aware of this aspect of AI. Be true to your own code of ethics and do the right thing when being creative. AI is a wonderful tool right up to the point that it is not.

My New AI Partner

I'm only just beginning to dabble in open-source AI, and I'm looking for more secure AI products that will allow me to maintain control of my intellectual property. Open-source AI can review your screenplay, novel, or business book manuscript for errors, insights, or as a sounding board based on themes and angles you'd hoped to address, but your material will become part of that open-source platform's database. Whoosh! Your unique creative insights are no longer unique.

This was alarming to me at first. However, this is the limitation and risk presented by the two-pound version of AI we get for free. It may cost a few dollars to get protected AI capabilities, but I think it's worth every penny. AI as a tool is an amenable partner, ready, willing, and able to enhance your personal productivity. As a writer, professional speaker, and consultant, gaining immediate critical feedback of my works in progress would be invaluable.

We started discussing AI in the context of creativity, and I want to come full circle back to the perceived threat to creativity AI represents. You are free to use or not use AI in your personal life. You or your employer may decide to bring AI into the workplace. AI isn't an entity stalking us, waiting for us to make a mistake. It is a program, albeit a generative self-learning program, designed to help. If you fear this, then you are already defeated.

AI will be able to connect the dots faster. This isn't intuition; it's programing. If it doesn't have access to all the dots, then it will not know its construct is flawed. Our role is to be always aware that AI is a tool and not magic. We will have to find (or create) the dots that make a difference, then introduce those insights into the database of human endeavor. AI will absorb and apply going forward, but we will still be the fountainhead of weird, odd, incredible, and awesome creative output.

I'll take this new thing for a test ride in the coming year and try to leverage AI as a tool in my creative work. A partner in innovation, not a movie monster. Standing tall and demanding change like AI to stop is self-defeating and futile. It would be like screaming in the street 20 years ago that handheld smart phones would destroy the world. Embrace through understanding. Learn and become adept. Seek ways to leverage AI and make it your partner in forging inspiring new outcomes. Be stronger, wiser, and smarter. *Be Different!*

Chapter Fifteen

Your Creative Team

Creativity is intelligence having fun.
Albert Einstein

Being a part of a creative group, striving to solve a significant challenge, is an amazing feeling. I participated in this as a Navy SEAL and repeatedly in my post-military career. I have great memories of joy, humor, tension, fear, and many other emotional experiences related to being a part of this dynamic. We didn't always win, or even come close sometimes, but the pursuit was exhilarating and rewarding.

To form a creative team, you need to address all the elements of human intellectual conflict noted in the earlier chapters of this book, on a person-by-person basis. This is to confirm all the participants you selected are truly and individually free to think without inhibition. Forming a group and labeling them as creative or innovative will not make them so. You need to screen each candidate for their intellectual humility, curiosity, and creative potential before assembling the team.

I read recently that a modern focus on teams drove the creation of teams that were anything but. Rather, committees of conflicted and closed-minded people pursuing personal and interorganizational agendas without risk of failure, voting on diplomatic outcomes designed not to wow, but to homogenize differences. This may sound overly critical, and perhaps it is; however, most teams in most organizations do not generate spectacular breakthroughs. How they are structured may be the reason.

Special operations teams are constructed with care based on lessons learned over time, influenced by current mission requirements and anticipated demands in the future. A few selection criteria are similar across the various specialized units, and some are unique to each. One consistent theme or point of view held by those responsible for training and leading special operators is that the approach to evaluating the raw material (the physical and psychological foundation of each individual) must stay consistent over time, even as mission requirements change.

This strongly held belief gets emotional quickly if someone tries to change this underlying premise—that all SEALs, Green Berets, Marine Raiders, or Air Force special operators can deal with the core challenges, regardless of where their missions take them. Technology changes, target geography changes, specific tasks change, but the quality of the people does not. Physical stamina, psychological resiliency, and individual and collective creativity combine to deliver maximum flexibility and a high probability for success.

I'm not suggesting you forge a special operations unit to succeed in your endeavors. My point is to drive home the need to recognize and develop the core principles of creativity and innovation in yourself and in your team. This will serve as a powerful foundation for your team of engaged professionals. Much like the special operations process, if you have the foundational behaviors in place, then your team will be nimble and open-minded enough to take on the tasks you give them in a creative and impactful manner. Their receptiveness will provide poise and illuminate more, rather than fewer, insightful solutions.

Profiles in Creativity

I make the case in my book *Be Visionary* that some people are just not into creative work. These are people who abhor risks, change, chaos, and melt down quickly under mild stress, let alone a crisis. In my book, I suggest identifying and leveraging those who have potential for creative work (the dreamers) and those who do not (the risk averse). I describe how to use both mindsets to achieve strategic aims, one group to shape the future and the other to vet and find flaws in the vision or creative logic. I still believe this is a productive way to get everyone involved in a key project.

In the military and in the SEAL Teams, you can't fire someone like you can in the commercial world. The rank and associated compensation is tied to tenure, testing, and annual evaluations. Once a vetted and selected person becomes a part of the unit, leaders have a sworn duty to develop them and steadily improve their expertise across multiple categories of performance. In the case of officers, it makes it more difficult to follow the advice presented in *Be Visionary* and that noted in the last paragraph.

All military leaders are required to exercise creativity, judgment, and at the same time moderate risks; but not all rise to the challenge. Most negative observations about midlevel and senior officers are related to imagination, intellectual maturity, and judgment. To successfully command in combat requires all three attributes. Therefore, as time rolls on, some officers rise through the ranks and other officers stop being promoted. The writing on the wall, many leave the military, a few decide to hold out as long as possible; but these men and women will never be given a command to lead.

In the early chapters of this book, I lay the responsibility to change your way of thinking squarely on your shoulders. Now I'm going to discuss how to help others do so. In my book *Be Nimble*, I explain how SEALs use scenario-based training to develop and hone combat leadership skills. This is the same method I suggest you use when developing creativity in people. First, you develop a profile of who you need in your team. You should begin with emotional maturity, a sense of humor, intellectual humility, a willingness to explore and listen, and the ability to leave the baggage of their experiences at the door. A team of people with these characteristics is ready to create, to think both broadly and narrowly.

Imagine this group in a room, addressing a challenge. No parochial points of view, only curiosity. No fixed philosophical position, only a desire to discover. A team that will take in and evaluate the known data inputs, while at the same time be willing to range far and wide to find other unknown data points and insights. Willing to experiment, model multiple possibilities, and merge divergent streams of thought into an effective hybrid solution. This is all possible, as long as the team is assembled with people fitting the creative profile.

Leading Creative Teams

If you plan to lead a creative team, then you must also have all the traits I've listed and one more—patience. Innovative thinking is a messy affair. You must not try to shape its outcome or overly influence the process of creativity. Otherwise, you will trigger the team member's underlying default to conformity and intellectual risk mitigation. If the team thinks you as the leader leans in a certain direction, prefers a certain path, they will realize the exercise is a farce or, even worse, a trap. If there is an unspoken right answer, then they will seek guidance from you as their leader to find that right answer instead of engaging in creative expression.

An example of this happens every day to leaders, albeit outside the paradigm of a creative team. Direct reports approach their leader to present a challenge. In most cases, these people have the authority to make the call themselves. They lay out the minute details of a problem, and, once finished, they shut up and stare at the leader, waiting for a reaction and a decision.

Why are they doing this? Why aren't they comfortable transitioning from problem definition to recommendations for action? You can probably answer this through personal experience. It's because they are worried that they will look stupid. Their fear of failure can be solved easily by having the boss produce a plan. It's a great insurance policy against the direct report's personal accountability. If the leader's plan fails, it falls on the leader, not the direct report.

Leading a creative team with a heavy hand will cause this same professional risk-aversion behavior. So how do you lead a creative team? You must first check your ego at the door and practice the same baggage shredding exercise noted earlier in this book. Next, you must define the outcome in clear language. Using a metric helps, but many challenges cannot be solved this way. Think what, not how to arrive at the goal statement. Any indication you give as to how it may be achieved has colored the creative pool with your intentions already.

Your team will let you know through their behaviors if you are invading their intellectual space or not. Any cessation of idea flow in your presence is a warning sign to back off. This is hard for most leaders, because most leaders make decisions for a living; they do not operate think tanks or academic research teams. Having the maturity and patience to let the creative process work itself out is a rare trait in a leader. It may take practice and time to become proficient, but you can learn this skill. Are you up to the task? If you are, then you are closer to being a different kind of leader and more likely to develop a truly innovative and successful team.

Internal Team Dynamics

The most awkward thing to do, related to creative teams, is to get the internal chemistry right. Think of all the musical groups over the decades who were highly innovative and talented, churning out hits and even timeless classics one after the other, only to suddenly implode and fade away. A musical group is a good comparison for our purposes here, because it requires a team of people to engage on many levels of creative inquiry, ideation, development, and implementation.

Bands that last the longest have a healthy respect for the abilities of their members and allow each person to express their talents. A drummer who can write great songs and play the keyboard won't be happy for long if only relegated to the drums. This is why many musical groups that have survived celebrate and highlight their multitalented bandmates on concert tours or on albums.

As discussed in the previous segment, overbearing team leadership has several pitfalls; so does allowing an alpha leader to emerge within the group. We've all seen this before. A little while into the life of a new team, someone becomes tired, bored, or frustrated, and feels the need to take charge. One way to avoid this is to follow my suggestions on the formation of your team; but if you can't be as deliberative and selective, then you will face the emerging alpha challenge.

What to do? Well, assuming the team has been assembled to solve problems specifically, or design solutions, services, or products, I suggest you reinforce the point of the exercise—diversity of intellect merged and combined purposefully to achieve something new. You don't have to rise to become an alpha yourself; as a mature participant, you simply need to nudge the process back to its open-minded path.

This is better accomplished by team or peer intervention, rather than a one-on-one countering effort. So if you see someone else in your team attempting to calm an alpha personality, weigh in and support them. Alpha personalities are much like playground bullies. Give them power over you and the process, and they will take more and more control until they are the de facto leader of the team. And if you are the alpha, think about the wonder of diverse and thoughtful exchange of ideas, and how that serves a higher purpose than a forcefully directed outcome. Take the high road and participate; don't dominate.

Managing and guiding people to a creative and constructive conclusion isn't an easy thing to do. Even without the alpha element, truly creative people are passionate people and that means high energy. Leading high-energy people takes patience and the right blend of firm directional influence and freedom to wander for a short time before locking in and moving on. If you learn how to do that well, you will be invaluable wherever you work. It's a practiced art that requires maturity and a thick skin.

The Value of Time Constraints

Not all projects lend themselves to abbreviated timeframes, but you can structure the sessions in a way that chunks each milestone of productive activity, breaking them down into smaller, bite-sized periods of creative effort. This is a key to melding ideation, compressing time to incite a sense of intellectual urgency. Given all the time in the world, people, creative people, will take it and roam endlessly. While this might be a fruitful academic methodology, it won't accomplish much of immediate value for the organization.

Performing with a sense of urgency also spurs chemical changes in the body. It stimulates the fight or flight response and gives the impression of rapidly approaching failure. Faced with this, most professionals rise to the occasion. Have you ever noticed what happens to the level of play in professional sports competitions as the clock winds down, leaving less and less time to affect the outcome? This is a very human reaction and one you should understand and tap into.

There is a cliché related to establishing a false sense of urgency. It is the often-cited idea of a boss handing an impossible task to a team in a room and leaving them to find the solution. As the boss departs, he or she tosses out, "Nobody's leaving until you've found an answer!" The door slams shut and the team stares at each other. Does this ever happen in the real world?

I've been a participant in multiple high-stakes proposal development events, where we were sequestered for 12 to 14 hours a day, weekends, nights, whatever it took to get the project finished and submitted on time. This was a true sense of urgency exercise. A fixed deadline, a huge task, a team, and the time remaining. I'm here to tell you we always thought the project wasn't going to be completed on time. We wasted the first hour complaining about the unfairness and the stupidity associated with the mandate and those who were dumb enough to issue it to us. Then we settled down and made it happen. Over and over again.

So, I'm skeptical when a team tells me they can't accomplish an urgent task. In 1942, C. Northcote Parkinson observed this challenge from a unique perspective. This perspective came to be known as Parkinson's Law. The law states that work expands to fill the time allotted for its completion. This was Parkinson's take on human nature. I've watched this unfold countless times, and I'm sure you have, too. My experience with the SEALs proved it over and over again.

Unlike movie and television depictions of elite combat missions, modern day commandos rarely execute the task precisely as planned. I was part of a target planning team for two years, focused on three separate sites. My platoon was assigned one of the three. For two years, we rehashed the plan, dismantled the plan, and rebuilt the plan. There wasn't a single detail that wasn't analyzed, evaluated, and weighed.

Finally, the day came when it was time to do the deed. We found ourselves going in, not with a plan; the last one had disintegrated as everything on the ground changed in the blink of an eye. All our assumptions went up in smoke, and we had 45 minutes to put a new plan together. It turns out this was reality in combat, even for elite troops. All the obsessing for two years, all the live rehearsals produced a plan that was no better or worse than what we conceived in those 45 minutes.

The key to this topic is the team and the quality of the professionals in that team. Staying on topic and on target regarding standards, time, and resources expended. Creating a false sense of urgency may be needed at times, but professionals selected to be involved in innovation normally do not need to be spurred forward to action using gimmicks. Be honest with them and set the time limits for production reasonably, unless the universe hasn't given you that luxury. Watch each member of the team to see who shines under time-related pressure and who folds.

This crucible of imagination and ingenuity while the clock is ticking is the only way you can observe this reaction. Training, mentoring, and coaching may change the dynamic; but if it doesn't, be sure you pick only stress eaters for the time-urgent projects. The true value added of either real or artificially imposed time constraints is an increased level of team energy and laser like focus on a successful collective output.

Have Fun

Business is serious, engineering is serious, medicine and law are serious endeavors; but sometimes even serious areas of work can be fun. Especially when we are trying to be creative. Albert Einstein's quote at the beginning of this chapter says it best. "Creativity is intelligence having fun." After everything I've said in this chapter, I think it's important to end on this note.

The people in the Navy SEALs, and those of our elite counterparts in the Army, Air Force, and Marines, are known within their elite communities as fun-seeking and lighthearted personalities. Joking is an elixir of joy in a world filled with stress and risk. A sense of humor, even in the direst of circumstances, is a must. Creating solutions to critical challenges, often without all the resources required or the time needed, is better performed with friendship, humor, and levity.

As a participant or a leader, you must believe in fun as the antidote to fatigue and pressure. Inject it as a break in the work, encourage it as a part of the work atmosphere; and even when things are as bad as they can be, smile. If you do, others will follow your lead. Be creative!

Chapter Sixteen

The Creative Cycle

I have not failed. I've just found 10,000 ways that won't work.
Thomas Edison

Trial and error, experimentation, and the creative cycle are never ending ... unless you decide to stand pat on the status quo. Big mistake. As noted throughout this book, stasis is not the way of the universe. Change is happening because of your behaviors or it's happening anyway, and you are riding the whirlwind. Reading about the rise and fall of empires and nations is enlightening and humbling, but seeing the results of this history firsthand is even more impactful.

As a teenager I used to walk the railways near my Uncle Gene's house in Sioux City, Iowa. I was an enthusiastic collector of beer cans. I went to swap meets where thousands of people gathered to trade, sell, or buy beer cans from all over the country and overseas. The rarest form of beer can was the cone top, an original can design that tapered at the top to look like a squat metal bottle. The cleaner the cone top, the more valuable.

As I walked along the lonely rail line, I found myself following a rail spur that went off into the woods, separating from the main line. As I walked, I became aware of small buildings scattered about the woods with rusty piles of metal laying nearby. I turned a corner and came to an abrupt stop. In front of me was an old factory. The woods had grown up around the facility, making it fascinating and spooky at the same time. I looked around, expecting to see evidence of people; but I was alone, completely alone.

It was an impressive brick structure at least five stories high. On the highest part of the building, written in script, were the words, "Falstaff Brewing Company." I vaguely remembered the name from my can collecting but wasn't sure I'd ever actually observed someone drinking the brew. Falstaff Brewing Company was once a great enterprise. Its origins began in 1840 in St. Louis, with production peaking in 1965. The brewing giant slowly declined until closing production in 2005.

What I found in the woods was representative of the beginning of the end. One of the far-flung production centers that were shut down one by one as Falstaff declined through the seventies and eighties until the brand became a mere shadow of its former glory. Of course, as I stood there staring at the brick brewery, I wasn't aware of this history, nor did I care. I had one thought—treasure! I scoured the facility over the span of a week.

On the fifth day, I struggled to pull back the corner of a huge canvas tarp I found covering a mound in the back of the structure. My multi-day exploratory efforts were rewarded by what I found under that tarp. Hundreds and hundreds of cone top Falstaff beer cans! The ones near the top and at the bottom of the pile were rusted or dented in such a way to be worthless. Ah, but the motherlode was the middle layer. I didn't have any way to carry my prize, so I went back to my uncle's house and brought back a wheelbarrow.

Eventually I was able to recover 20 or so quality cone tops. At the end of the summer, I went back home to Omaha and began attending local beer can swap events. Some I sold and some I traded for other exotic cans. Each Falstaff cone top was worth 30 to 60 dollars. A hefty sum for a teenage kid working multiple jobs at seven bucks an hour. This story is a commercial one. A story of rise and fall. I've read so many stories of companies going through this boom-to-bust cycle that it feels natural. Not so much tragedy as inevitability. My journeys overseas would confirm this perspective.

My first overseas trip was to Japan. I toured the castles, the religious sites, and went to the historical museum in Tokyo. Later I would visit another 43 countries and do much the same thing. I toured every historical site I could, seeing the remnants of empires and nations. France, Spain, Germany, Greece, Italy, Israel, Iraq, Britain, and even Carthage, the ancient home of Hannibal the great general who nearly destroyed the Roman empire. What I realize now is these too represent the natural order of the universe. Change is inevitable. Life, business, and empires experience a cycle of experience. Many are protracted by force of will and intellect, many are not. Let's dive into this cyclical phenomenon a bit more.

Are We the Problem?

If the universe abhors stability and humans love stability, then it may be that we are the problem. Rather than make peace with the way things are, we hope to secure a place of unchanging quiet through imposition of controls, controls designed to impede and impair change. After a lifetime, professionals, who already have a very human desire to reside in a calm and controlled environment, accept and embrace organizational controls as sensible and righteous.

I hope by now you can see the folly in this. Spitting into the wind will not make a tornado stop being a tornado. Our puny measures to evade the inevitable chaos of steady or radical change are insufficient to affect the ultimate outcome. Far better that we strive to understand the forces that sway us personally, professionally, economically, and physically. For in doing so, we learn to surf the flow of reality and, better yet, anticipate the trends that are sure to disrupt our naïve fortress of intellectual and emotional denial.

Was the fall of Rome or the disintegration of the Dutch, Spanish, French, British, and German empires foreseeable? I can only assume the answer is yes. Is there evidence these social and economic constructs were aware of what was happening? Did they act and fail to stem the tide of change, or did they ignore the macro trends and hope to hold on to the status quo? What about the leadership of Falstaff Brewing? Kodak? BlackBerry? What about every defunct company that made the products we all loved, but are gone today? Did they see it coming?

Human nature is a powerful thing. Much of our success as a species is rooted in our ability to survive. That trait indicates to me that we've failed to see disaster coming, both small and large in scale, for hundreds of thousands of years. If our early ancestors were adept at creative long-range planning and flexible enough to turn hard left when the universe threw them a curve, then we wouldn't have needed a high ability to survive.

What we need to do, what you need to do, is accept the change premise and roll with it. What do you have to lose? If you lift your head up from the day-to-day grind of living and, worse, thinking inside the white lines painted for you by others, you just might see the train coming straight at you in time to step off the tracks calmly.

Can Behavior Affect the Inevitable?

The Catholic theologian and philosopher Saint Thomas Aquinas posited that human will is free, but only insofar as the intellect is free to make or revise judgments. In other words, humans have the gift of free will so they can decide. That puts the responsibility for action or inaction on the individual, not another person, and not an institution or organization. From this perspective we all have the capacity to decide differently one day to the next and one change event to the next. Then why do so few leaders behave in a way that exercises free will when faced with the unknown?

I tend to side with Saint Thomas Aquinas. I believe we are born with free will, and, fortunately or not, it puts the monkey square on our back. I also believe the deer in the headlight's dilemma is the root cause of so many missed opportunities to get out of the way or to seize the window of opportunity. This applies to life as well as other productive endeavors. Learn to decide and you will be free to exercise your intellectual capabilities to affect outcomes.

There is an adage that delaying resolution or execution of an important issue will convert that issue from important to urgent. Then if the issue is ignored further, it soon becomes an emergency. Procrastination is often a symptom of one's failure to exercise their gift of free will in a timely manner, coupled with a wrongheaded desire to preserve stability as the prime directive. In the end, a compelling challenge will be dealt with one way or another. Just ask the Romans.

Cycle Theory

Cycle theory is based on the premise that what goes around comes around. In retrospect, it seems more principle than theory. The aforementioned great empires suffered the same process of rise, plateau, and fall. Economies, countries, businesses, and individuals all fall into this cyclical profile. If taken the wrong way, this could give one a sense of foreboding. If what goes up must come down, why bother in the first place? I beg to differ with this pessimistic view.

When I managed investments at UBS, I had the responsibility to track not only my high-net-worth clients' portfolios, but also track the greater investment environment. Think of moving across the Great Plains in the nineteenth century, wagons filled with all your possessions and your precious family. While you would certainly be aware of the details of your horses, wagons, and family, you would be insane not to be focusing most of your attention on the hills around you.

This was my mindset. Know and understand the dynamics related to the companies in my stock portfolios, but watch the horizon. This market-related situational awareness exercise provided me with an early warning system against surprise cyclical changes, for better or for worse. As I watched and observed different sectors of the economy rise and fall, I got a sense of the game. Like noting the tides, I was able to anticipate when and where to be financially based on these micro cycles. The economy writ large was also cyclical and more akin to a storm rising or abating. This level of cyclical event would in turn affect all the micro cycles.

In combat operations, there is a battle rhythm, a cycle of intensity, sustainment, and then lulls in activity. Historians write of this across the ages of warfare. Smart noncommissioned officers in the military teach it to new recruits. Nobody on either side of the battle lines can be on the attack forever. One side's pause is another side's opportunity and so on. Knowing this cycle allows military leaders to exploit and leverage the pace and trends to their advantage. Get to know the cycles that impact your world. They will be different and dependent on several factors, but they are discoverable and should be studied.

From a creative point of view, consider what your competition is doing right now. Are they surging sales and marketing outreach, building infrastructure, or laying off employees? If any of these is the case, what's next? Typically, overextension leads to pullbacks and downsizing of both activity and headcount. Anticipate that and see how you can plan on shooting in when your competition is pulling back.

Do you *feel* the calm before the AI storm? I certainly do. This will be a macro trend for several decades on par with creation of the Internet and cellular phones. I was around back then and nobody, I mean nobody, on the street cared about the Internet. Cell phones were too big and too expensive to be mainstream. In fact, if you had traveled back from the future and told me to invest in Microsoft, I would have thought you were crazy. Macro trends are our friends. Seek them out, understand them, and then think of ways they can improve your world. Become cycle aware!

Maintaining the Upward Cycle

A key question is at what point in a cycle are we. Another is what cycles matter to us personally, professionally, or organizationally. When I say organizationally, I mean as a species, a global collection of friends and allies, as a nation, and as a microcosm of that nation. Private or public in nature. For the sake of this segment, let's assume you find yourself on an upward trend in a cycle. It would be important to identify that cycle's history and specifically the duration of its trends over time. We know tides cycle multiple times a day. What about economic depressions? Or how small stocks move up and down over time as a class of investments?

Your chosen cycle may operate like the tides or more like macroeconomic shifts; but it will have a pattern, and it is the pattern that informs you of potential positive and negative probabilities. Falling in love with an upward cycle feels wonderful, but it is a fool who takes the ride all the way to the top. Sustaining upward momentum isn't about holding on for the ride; instead, it's about knowing when to leap off and onto another upward trend.

I like to imagine jumping off these cyclic elevators as they reach the eighteenth floor of a twenty-floor building in exchange for an elevator moving from the third to the fourth floor. Seasoned investors do this in real estate, commodities, gold, silver, and of course, stocks. Anyone working in any industry can become a student of their cycles and trends, and begin to leverage this insight to plan for a different future. If being innovative is to anticipate and seize the next normal, tracking these upward movements can be essential to success.

What to Do about Downward Cycles

As you might expect, there is a negative feeling about the idea of a trend diminishing, but what if that trend was related to a high incidence of hurricanes? There may be an element of peril and reward in everything; however, it's understanding the nuance of these rhythms that gives us an edge. Downward cycles of negative forces are natural and should be celebrated and embraced for the data they provide. They signal a change in the status quo, and that, my friend, means opportunity.

So, if you pay attention, then you will participate in the upward trends and defend against the downward trends, unless the downward trend removes or reduces risk, as in the case of historically severe weather. In the investment markets, people have ways to buy instruments that anticipate upward movement (therefore making money) while others anticipate downward movement (again making money). What about the end of technology trends? Or social trends? Sometimes the downward cycle is the death of a multi-year trend.

Fashion often works in this way. A thing is attractive and in great demand until it isn't. Usually, another fashion catches wind, and we all run to buy those clothes, shoes, hats, etc. In recent years, fashion has trended backward in time. Instead of new creative ideas blowing us away, fashion leaders have been simply copying fashions of the past. This is why we see young people walking around in 2023 dressed like it is 1970. Study both upward and downward cycles to know the full rotation over time. You can surprise your friends and coworkers with your prophetic awareness of what's going to happen next and, more importantly, what to do about it.

Leaning Forward

Cycles give us a path to understanding. As a species we were once in tune with the cycles of our environment. We knew when to plant, when to harvest, and when the seasons changed. We observed the cycle of life from birth to death. In present day America these natural processes remain, but our awareness of them is muted. There's not much we can do to disrupt the changing of the seasons or the cycle of life, but we can anticipate change and interact with other important cycles.

Creativity is one of many behaviors you will need to solve the challenges you face each day. The most innovative plan devised in a vacuum of environmental awareness will fail when reality changes lanes on you. Being the most inventive, the most imaginative, the most visionary thinker is moot unless the greater context of history is considered. Cycle theory can help you with that context. Nothing is guaranteed, but the combination of applied creativity and cycle awareness can help you leapfrog the naysayers and competition.

So why not accept the theory and use it as you contemplate your design? If you are part of or are leading a creative team, make sure you inject cycle theory into your deliberations. Remember, from the standpoint of forward knowledge, the trend is your friend. Will you be able to stop a trend that is threatening you or your organization? Probably not, at least not the macro trends. The small trends, like employee tardiness or poor communication, can be neutralized; but the trends that impact and influence industries, markets, and nations are difficult if not impossible to reverse. That's why you must lean into the trends, ride the cycles, and engineer a path to opportunity.

Can you start a cycle or trend? Of course you can, and thousands of people have over the centuries. Alas, history rarely reveals the origin story of ancient trends and cycles, with the exception of religions, in the last two thousand years. If your invention or innovation is so new, so fresh, and so compelling that it starts a cycle, congratulations! That is after all the point of this book. Having the faith and confidence in the power of your unencumbered mind to change the world for the better.

I'm a huge fan of cycle theory and know this helps me every day as I sift through the firehose blast of data points and messaging. It helps me to "see" around corners and over the horizon. It provides a backdrop of truth that aids me in positioning change. I encourage you to seek more information on this aspect of creative insight. Look around and watch the trends and cycles in motion. Use this, leverage this, make cycle theory a part of how you think about the universe operating all around you. Remember, it's far better to surf the trend than to be crushed by it!

Chapter Seventeen

Divergent Thought Leadership

A discerning mind pursuing divergent thinking is the crucible that stews creativity and meaning in life.
Abhinav Saxena

If you seek to be different and you accept the premise that to be different you must think differently, then you are already ten steps down the path of intellectual creativity. When I experienced firsthand the innovation of Vietnam-era SEALs, I took such thinking for granted. I was young, so I hadn't formed a personal philosophy about how I should apply my mind to a task. It was easy to adopt the processes of fact collection, analysis, solution design, and execution from those enlightened warriors. Their philosophy became my core operating system.

Plato, da Vinci, our founding fathers, the Beat Poets of the 1950s, Picasso, Steve Jobs, Elon Musk, and, yes, those Vietnam SEALs are only a few examples of the hundreds, perhaps thousands, of groundbreaking or rule-bending thinkers. During their lives, they interacted with our world in an impactful way by thinking differently. The labels *thought leader* or *influencer* are haphazardly bandied about today in social media, making these lofty characterizations appear mainstream.

While it's nice to be called a thought leader, it only takes one a few minutes of research into any true mental maven to feel humbled in comparison. Humble is good. Humble makes us hungry to learn more, to be more, to contribute more. In my opinion, thought leadership is where you find it, even if social media isn't yet aware of your insights. Anyone can be such an influencer. Maybe it's a small act of kindness, for even a smile can change a person's day.

The simple things do count. We can nudge a depressed soul toward emotional recovery just by the way we interact. We can provide the key insight that cracks open someone's personal or professional dilemma. By being different, all of us can make things different. First you need to take charge of your thoughts, *your* mind. You need to directly and positively influence your intellectual choices to steer away automatic obedience to imposed structures of creative oppression. You need to get your mental act together so you can start leading and contributing on a higher plane. Do this first, and you too can become a divergent thought leader.

Positive Divergence

I stress again that my approach to divergence is intellectual, and my intention is to affect positive change. However, what is positive for one person might be perceived by another as a negative. When my thought paper was turned into a new mission capability in my last few years in the SEAL Teams, I never suspected there would be those in that organization who would feel bitter as a result. This story is just one example of how good intentions, creative intentions, still may cause unforeseen collateral damage.

My concept was to turn our minisubs into delivery platforms for SEAL snipers. Up to that point, their designed application was to sink warships. I was sent to one of the special teams servicing this capability and all hell broke loose. What I didn't know was these units were full of old frogmen who loved diving and anything related to diving technology. Especially the old guard, the senior enlisted and warrant officers, who on average had 20 years in the Navy and over ten years working with the minisubs.

Much of the countermovement was led by this group, wholly based on their misconceptions, wrongheaded or not, which created a very real obstacle to achieving what I'd been tasked to accomplish. It took a few months to discover this source of subtle sabotage and confront it. I spent hours on runs, in bars, in conference rooms, trying to persuade these men to relax a bit and give the vision of a new future a chance. In hindsight, there's no doubt the initiative was the right thing to do. It literally saved these units from being decommissioned and gave them a new life related to the new role. Still, however noble this thought leadership project was, opposing perceptions of my conceived value proposition caused problems for several years.

In the media, divergence is applauded and edgy, almost spiritual, magical. It is associated with artists and people distorting the static present with breakthrough insights. All good, right? What isn't as apparent is the opposition to this way of thinking. It's all joy and awe and no downside. I'm here to tell you that's never the case. I wouldn't tell you to stop thinking to avoid the angst of others; I only want you to be dialed in to the unintended consequences.

In my experience, you may not get credit for the thoughtful initiative you champion. You may only get to fight the pushback, struggle with the ramp-up while being ostracized by coworkers. This is because change takes time and change creates chaos. It took a full three years for that minisub mission redo to be up and running as an accepted capability, and many other change management projects in business were successful long after I left the organization. I don't feel like a martyr because of this history; on the contrary, I now know all the pain and suffering was worth it. Positive change was the result of my and others' commitment to make things better.

The Price of Leadership

Being an active thought leader will place you squarely in the bull's-eye socially. I've shared multiple experiences in this book about the price I paid to be different. Regardless of hindsight feelings of accomplishment, when I was in the moment it was rough. I say this because you will need courage to step up and strike a creative pose amongst your inhibited and risk-adverse coworkers or management peer group. Intellectual rebels have always been subjected to ridicule, shaming, and social isolation. It comes with the territory.

If you stay the course and maintain your poise under this social pressure to conform and not rock the boat, then you will inevitably attract like-minded people who, having heard your vision, will decide to jump on the innovation yacht with you. As with all leadership, this should be understood as a responsibility. Your creative movement should be organized and led as a positive contribution to improvement. This aspect of thought leadership is no different than standard leadership. Be constructive, respectful, and thoroughly prepared at all times to demonstrate your ideas dispassionately and diplomatically.

Detractors will look for weakness, flaws in your process, your concepts. There are always people who get their kicks from tearing down rather than building up. Even these people deserve your attention. Like bullies everywhere, these naysayers feed on emotional reactions to their poking and prodding. Don't give them that satisfaction. Stand tall and smile, even during the worst moments. As a thought leader you need to set an example for those who support and follow you. Meanness will be observed and replicated, so set the tone and establish the communications method.

These tips also apply to thought leaders who project their inspiration and philosophy by social media, speaking, or authoring books. While you can't see your adherents, they are absorbing your message and the way you convey that message. If you are rude, blunt, aggressive, and arrogant, your followers will adopt the same posture. I think about this when I write, because I've seen incredibly gifted influencers disregard this advice in order to appear edgy or to inflame passion in their constituents. Take the high road and don't lead through drama, bullying, and resistance. Do it in style and grace. Be a true thought leader.

Communications and Messaging

One of the most difficult aspects of thought leaders, or any form of leadership for that matter, is communication. Part substance, part style, communicating change management driven by innovative energy requires a nuanced approach. When a leader tells someone to do a task and that task is a standard and well-known activity, there is little to no intellectual or emotional pushback. However, when you lay out your plan to change the world, you'd better be ready to deal with the consequences. Questions, some heated, some muted, but always emotional and self-centered. That is a natural human reaction and therefore the natural outcome of your actions. Expect this and prepare accordingly.

Being a good communicator is key to winning over converts, diffusing disagreements, and rallying resources. Being good at crafting the message is just as important. Even the most difficult of messages, say telling someone a family member has died, can be improved by the way the message is delivered. In my experience, most thought leaders are not especially good at either of these skills. There are exceptions, and these people are highly effective at changing minds, hearts, and influencing creative change. This is the type of thought leader you should strive to be.

So, what's in a convincing message? To start with, the core must be an answer to the question why. Why go through the turmoil, chaos, and angst always associated with significant adjustment to the status quo? Why now, why us, and why not wait? You must anticipate this line of spoken or unspoken inquiry as you draft the words you will say or write describing the audacious initiative. The next concern will be about who will be impacted. Nobody overreacts to a major facelift in somebody else's business division. That's why you need to be specific and factual in your messaging; don't pull punches. Be candid, direct, and then lay on your view of the future after the change is implemented.

Selling the Vision

In my opinion, candor without candy makes for a sour conversation. Most self-described thought leaders in the media don't have the burden of pulling and pushing others along to the conclusion of their inspiring idea. Many pontificate and write lofty thought pieces without the responsibility of real-world ramifications. However, if you are a professional in an organization you will have to deal with reality. Selling the vision is the icing on the fact-filled cake. You need to inspire and ignite fresh energy, energy many will have forgotten they had within themselves.

You'll need to point to the horizon and paint a picture they can all see and understand. A picture of success, improvement, and new opportunities—not just for the organization, but for each of them, too. You don't have to be a thespian or a professional speaker to accomplish this. Just be passionate and honest. The truth of what you believe will come through loud and clear.

Loudly or softly, lay it all out and leave nothing unsaid. Answer questions until they stop coming. Then set the schedule for your initiative and ask everyone for their help and advice going forward. One by one you will overcome objections and forge a coalition of believers. I decided to write this chapter for practical reasons. Creativity and innovation are bandied about by academics and social media influencers without substance, without practical experience in the trenches making dreams come true.

It's not enough for these talking heads to recite mere song lyrics or display sheet music to the crowd. This is all sizzle and no steak. To effectively pull all that artistic energy and potential together, you need musicians, and those musicians need to gel as a team. This is inspirational thought as implemented outcome. Not poetry or shallow commentary. As a thought leader, you should not be satisfied with soap box pontification. You should strive to convert inspiration into a concept, a concept into a plan, and a plan into something tangible that makes a positive difference. Don't get me wrong, I love poetry; but we're trying to change the world here, not impress a date.

I'd venture to say that outlining a practical progression to those you wish to influence sets you apart as a thought leader. Most people are comfortable throwing out an idea or a criticism, but few have the courage and commitment to see the thing through to the end. Leaders have this ability; and if you want to lead innovation, then you have to embrace the entire change management process, soup to nuts. Will it be easy? The simple answer is no. By now you understand that any force of will or focused thought leadership that challenges the way things are will be met with resistance. Are you up to the task? Can you be more than a shallow influencer and take the steps necessary to make good things happen? Learn to sell the vision and then lead that vision!

Chaos Is Natural—Plan for It

Divergent thinking is just that, thought. Divergent thinking converted into physical action has consequences. So far, I've focused on the positive outcomes of thought leadership; now it's time to discuss the potential downside for an organization. All leadership carries the burden of moral and ethical conduct. Evil leaders decide to ignore the conventions of society and nations; bad leaders do so to a lesser degree, only ignoring the norms where and when it suits their purpose.

Good leaders strive to lead while adhering to and maintaining an ethical and moral posture. Their case—if chaos and crisis is the result of their benevolent actions, it isn't on purpose. Evil, bad, or good, leaders effect change; and as a good leader, you need to be prepared to clean up the negative consequences of your actions. In truth, the universe isn't concerned with maintaining things as they are. Our world is in a constant state of evolution and devolution. Businesses, organizations, cities, nations, they all are subject to this never-ending process of adaptation. As professionals we understand that, and as a leader you train and prepare for that reality. However, incompetence and dumb luck also can create madness and mayhem.

When making changes large and small, I aspire to follow the maxim of the famous Greek scholar and healer Hippocrates: *First, do no harm.* This line, now referred to as the Hippocratic oath, sums up my organizational design philosophy along with the adage: *Measure twice and cut once.* Twin guidelines I've used for 20 years. I consider them when I develop strategy, operating plans, or when I must reorganize to scale up or down. I use them when I consider my options regarding hiring, firing, and promoting talent. Sounds simple, and for me it works. In a multiphase plan of any length, I assess each phase and outcome using these two rules.

So back to chaos and crisis. One is a natural part of the change process. People get confused for a while as their tasks shift, functions are redesigned, leadership is moved around, and standards of performance are upgraded. Just moving someone from one floor to another can be perceived as chaos by that person. Chaos is in the eye of the beholder.

Knowing this will be the case, thought leaders need to bake the friction and resistance of natural chaos into their planning expectations. Saying all employees will wear green jerseys versus red jerseys starting on Monday is easy to say, but be prepared for the chaos on Monday and be patient. Change takes more time for some to accept than for others. A rapid progression from normal to new normal violates the Hippocratic oath. First do no harm.

I'm impulsive when it comes to designing change management, and I'm impatient when it comes to implementing that change. Delays of any kind upset me and cause frustration. I can't help it; it's how I'm wired. However, I've learned by bitter personal experience that this personality trait of mine is counterproductive. I've learned to understand the effects of change on people and on organizations.

My impulsiveness led me to start plans without measuring twice; hell, in my early career, I didn't measure at all! I was like the great Civil War Navy Squadron commander, David Farragut. During the 1864 battle of Mobile Bay, he commanded his ships to attack, ignoring the explosive mines floating all around (called torpedoes at the time). He shouted his famous command, "Damn the torpedoes, full speed ahead!" This was my personal maxim during my early leadership years. Damn the consequences, just go, go, GO!

War is a change agent. Conflict on any scale destroys what is and alters the reality of those subjected to its disruption. Humans always rebuild as much as they can, and usually in an effort to restore their past normalcy. But as human beings, we never really get back to the sense of comfort and safety we may have enjoyed prior to the conflict. Larger scale events, civil wars, regional wars, and global wars may influence every aspect of our lives forever, making it impossible to go back. In these scenarios, the rebuild is forward-looking and transformative.

I've been a student of military history since I was 14, and of course I served as a SEAL for 20 years. I seek answers from that history that I believe translate to nonmilitary situations for two reasons. First, wars are historical, and as such they are recorded. The adversaries, the generals, the back and forth until victory or defeat. These are laid down through the ages, from the stone monuments erected by the Hittites describing the Battle of Kadesh against the Egyptians 3300 years ago to the conflict raging in Ukraine as I write this book.

Businesses through human history have not recorded their histories in the same detailed or comprehensive manner. The study of warfare includes statesmanship, economics, communications, organizational design, strategy, alliances, and much more. All areas of human activity that are consistent with nonmilitary organizations. The second reason I study military history is to understand human nature. Human beings have not changed much biologically or emotionally over the last few thousand years. Reading how the ancient Greeks chose dictatorship over democracy because of a looming external threat is priceless information about how we individually and collectively react to crisis and instability.

Case in point in recent time is the global COVID-19 pandemic. Nations around the world, even democracies with liberal freedoms of expression, movement, and choice regarding personal health decisions, were suddenly taking those freedoms away, justified by the big threat. The similarity throughout human history in such cases is compelling. To become an exceptional thought leader, you need to become a student of humanity, and that means becoming a student of history.

The old saying *history repeats itself* is misleading. Human nature repeats itself, and that is the key not only to understanding the past but also the future. Your thought leadership will set in motion changes that will follow a course we've all experienced personally and historically. Fear followed by confusion. Frustration followed by resistance, then acceptance and calm. Know this to be true and plan for this all too human inevitability. Be poised and comforting. Don't expect or demand acceptance and obedience on day one. Allow for this progression in your timeline and make sure your communications and messaging reiterate the vision and the promise of their efforts.

Human Nature Is the Key

When I was the chief petty officer in charge of the first phase of basic SEAL training, I was invited to a meeting that changed what America knew about the Navy's secret warriors. It was before books and movies about SEALs. My parents didn't have a clue what I did, and that was the directive. However, the new president wanted to expand all special operations forces, and the SEALs had been ordered to increase their manpower by 350. That order represented a doubling of the SEAL community. The meeting was about how to make that happen.

At the time, seventy-five percent of all SEAL candidates came from Navy ships. Sailors volunteering for the chance to become commandos. Most of the remaining twenty-five percent were family or friends of SEALs serving or who had served. We had no Navy recruiting program, no recruiting materials, and no recruiting video. After hours of heated debate (mass producing elite fighters and telling the world about SEALs was anathema to our code and our DNA), we settled down to watch the only piece of Navy video ever produced on the SEALs. Originally a briefing tool for senior Navy and civilian leaders, *Men with Green Faces* was a boring, poorly edited attempt to explain what a SEAL did.

As I listened to the post screening debate, I realized that only updating and refreshing that film was a mistake. There were 20 leaders in that conference room, and we were well into our fourth hour of fruitless whining and complaining. I was by far the most junior person there, and so I held my tongue. But eventually I had to say what was going through my mind. The briefing film was all boats and logs. Running on sand and pushups. It was all about the basic course experience, not about being a SEAL. I knew what I was about to say would mark me as a loon; but being young and somewhat ignorant of the dynamics at play, I opened my mouth, and it changed things in a big way.

I started by saying we've been twisting and wiggling on the hook for three hours to no good purpose. Nobody wants to say anything about the SEALs, but to simply reproduce an outdated film about punishment wouldn't inspire anyone to volunteer. I brought up a recent Marine Corps recruiting television ad that was a departure from their traditional straightforward message. In the television ad, a young man was chased by an unseen force intent to do harm. He climbed a rocky cliff and found a sword at the top. Thrusting the sword into the air, he transformed into a Marine in full dress uniform and rifle. The words "The few, the proud, the brave, United States Marines," appeared on the screen.

I finished my outburst by saying we needed an emotional message to drive the numbers we need into the pipeline. If we had a hoard of volunteers flowing in, we wouldn't have to lower standards to meet the president's goals. Show them the light at the end of the tunnel; don't focus on the selection process. The room of older and more experienced SEALs was quiet. I was absolutely sure I was going to be lambasted for my naïve idea, but nobody said a word. Our commanding officer looked at his watch and cleared his throat. All eyes shifted to him. "I think Chief Strong has explained our situation. We have our orders. I also think he's right. We need a different approach. That's all for now, thank you."

I got up and turned to leave with the rest of the leadership, but the commanding officer asked me to stay. I sat back down and was concerned again. I'd only been a chief for two months. Was I about to get dressed down for my impudence? To my surprise, I was put in charge of the new recruiting movie. Storyboarding my idea, writing a script for the narration, everything. It was eventually called *Someone Special* and was produced in over ten languages for the next 20 years, only being replaced shortly after the attacks on 9/11/2001, when another president asked for more SEALs.

I share this story to illustrate the point that human nature is consistent, and understanding human nature helps us as thought leaders to shape the narrative in a way that leverages positive human energy, drive, ambition, and aspiration for a better tomorrow. I didn't understand this at the time, but what my idea had leveraged was the Marine Corps' insight into human motivation. They didn't want volunteers looking for a way to get college paid for or to sightsee around the world. They wanted warriors. The television ad was groundbreaking and phenomenally successful. The recruiting movie *Someone Special* was also a hit and successful for the same reason. SEALs are warriors at heart. Not heroes or celebrities, warriors. That ethos is about honor, sacrifice, commitment, and a willingness to defend others, even if the price is life or limb. Communicate the vision, implement the vision, be a thought leader of divergent and exciting change; but always be aware of the human factor. Lead on!

Chapter Eighteen

The Future Is Today

The future cannot be predicted, but futures can be invented.
Dennis Gaber

My first exposure to a professional futurist was when I read a book entitled *The Popcorn Report*. The author, Faith Popcorn, was a proven source of business wisdom at the time. She combined instinct, historical context, demographic trends, and logic to arrive at remarkably accurate predictions about the future of society, economics, and business. I was struck by the simplicity of her approach and of her reliance on a keen understanding of human nature.

Later I became a huge fan of Harry Dent, famous for his demographic and statistical analysis of how the Baby Boomers had impacted the American business landscape and would continue to do so for decades. His book *The Roaring 2000s* was a must-read for financial professionals and retail businesses. It was these two soothsayers who guided me to my method of interpreting tea leaves. As noted in the last chapter, history and human nature are the pillars of that method.

While I don't claim to be a futurist, I spend an inordinate amount of time gazing dreamily into that shiny unknown realm. A place where nothing has happened, *so anything can happen.* People often are chastised for living in the past. It makes sense, because it is in the past where most of our sense of self resides. It is where all our memories are stored, some wonderful and others not so great.

Think Like a Novelist

An exercise I like to engage in from time to time is what I call Future Think. It's easy to play and only requires the suspension of disbelief. In other words, try not to be too serious when practicing this method. I begin by purging my active mind of past and present concerns, challenges, and social and interpersonal difficulties. I don't meditate as much as change the plane of my thinking. It's a game of what if, and why not, that can last a few minutes or a few hours. I take immense joy in doing this every so often, and incidentally it's this practice that led me to writing a successful series of time traveler novels.

If you think about it for a moment, novelists and screen writers must create a world and characters who live in that world. For the sake of this discussion let's stick to creative work focused on fantasy, science fiction, or alternate realities. Writers of these genres must disengage from the mundane and repetitive normality of everyday life so they can paint a new reality with words. One thing I've found as a novelist is that it was far easier to write the four books in my time travel series than it was to write the five books in my SEAL series. The difference was hard reality versus contrived reality. One is logical and anchored in truth, the other is fanciful.

A novelist and a futurist paint from the same palette. What should the world look like in the future? Will it be a natural slow progression of climate, social changes, technology advancements, or will it be a lurching and tumultuous roller coaster ride of dramatic readjustment? How do you play this guessing game in the first place? Well to let you off the hook, the answer is it doesn't matter. Nobody's watching and no one knows what the future holds, so why worry about it? Just sit down with a cup of coffee, stare out of the window, and begin.

Macro Trends

We've discussed trends in previous chapters, and instinctively you know these major tidal changes can modify things for all of us, often in every category of life. Climate is a good example. Our planet's climate has been cycling for eons. Core samples taken in the Arctic display the heating, cooling, and reheating of our planet multiple times over millions of years. Our ancient human ancestors couldn't stop it; nor can we. To ignore it is silly, so we will all adjust and adapt when the time comes, just like a thousand generations before us.

Human learning, and the enlightenment that follows, also has experienced waves of improvement, evolution, and collapse. One hundred years ago, the span of recorded history was defined by the Old Testament of the Bible, estimated at around 3500 years BCE. The study of archaeology and advancements in technology related to that discipline have extended our understanding much further back in time. In 2016 in southern Africa, the remains of multiple burials were found deep in a cave. Bodies were ritually placed in oval depressions and covered. A stone tool was found in the hand of one small figure and on the walls were etchings. The first evidence of an attempt to record an event, 250,000 years ago!

My takeaway from this mind-blowing discovery is that we humans and our prototypical cousins don't know what we don't know about the length of our historical progression and the number of innovative cycles we've experienced over hundreds of thousands of years. Before the discovery of this cave in Africa, the oldest evidence of ritual burial dated 80,000 years ago. What happened in the intervening time? Was there a renaissance of human activity, building and developing better and more specialized tools? If so, what happened next? Did something occur that set us back as a species?

Why am I focusing on the past in a chapter about the future? I think you know the answer. The future isn't always a ramp to greater and greater knowledge and achievement. Often it is a reversal of advancement, a regression. As you ponder the macro possibilities forward in time, be sure to consider this possibility. As they used to tell me in the investment business, "Marty, trees don't grow into the clouds!" There are limits, and many times, as evidenced by human experience, there is backsliding.

Projecting Big Changes

There are a few different ways to think about the future. The first is the good old linear and logical extension of past experiences and performance out to the horizon. This may mean a downward trend will go on as far as your mind can see. Or an upward trend will race upward without pause. Or a flat trajectory will rule the day. I label these three gross directional possibilities trends A, B, and C, for the purposes of analysis and strategic planning.

Of course, my simple labeling method doesn't consider nuances or deviations to the three paths forward. There are surely hybrid trajectories you could and should contemplate. We all have diverse ways to muse about things; mine is a combination of deep free thinking and a whiteboard. As noted in my comparison to a professional writer's method, I need to crystalize my thoughts in graphic detail.

First, I think about which path I want to analyze first. Let's say I decide a linear extension of the past up to the present is my first choice. I label it A, then spend a few hours running scenarios through my mind related to everything continuing without variation. I consider the risks, threats, and opportunities. I evaluate my organization's capacity and capabilities to match that future path. Do we have the talent, the resources, the planning to not only cope, but also to thrive in this future projection?

Then I locate a white board and diagram path A. I load it with a timeline extending out no less than 24 months, and no longer than 48 months. I make notes regarding all the planning considerations, and, finally, I make a statement about my personal opinion regarding the probability of path A and the other assumptions I've made related to that path. I take a digital picture and start thinking about the next major trend possibility.

Once I've performed this deep-thinking, diagramming process, I print out the digital images of my work and pull in my operational brain trust. From this point on, I facilitate debate and discourse. Instead of owning any one path, I stay neutral and see where the collective thinking leads us. Inevitably, I will learn about micro trends or even macro trends that the team feels indicate the path that is evolving. I also get exposed to a far more granular level of risks, threats, opportunities, and resource challenges.

The wonderful thing about this exercise is it is just that; it's an exercise. A thought experiment about what the future might hold with no downside. As a thought leader, you have addressed the importance of facing the unknown with clarity and resolve. You also have helped mentor your team in the methodology of future think. After several of these events, your team will begin to *think in the future*, instead of the past. Of course, eventually you will have to come to grips with all the scenarios and pick one to plan for. Planning forward without contemplating all the possible outcomes is like driving one hundred miles an hour down a winding country road while staring in the rearview mirror. Avoid this fate, anticipate the future, and act!

Micro Trends

Anticipating the future can be accomplished in another way, by looking at micro trends happening all around us. To contrast this exercise with the last one discussed, imagine the life cycle of your teenage daughter from birth, through adolescence, onward to a career as a macro trend. The fact that she keeps violating your curfew a little more each time, weekend after weekend, is an example of a micro trend. The first represents a natural cycle we are all aware of. The second is more subtle, yet it points to trouble ahead.

Professional poker players speak of tells, small physical traits and mannerisms displayed by their opponent that communicate a particular mental state. The universe exhibits these hints in a similar manner. Each area of human activity, every industry, every market, every company all show their stripes. If you are aware and conscious of these environmental messages, if you tune in and focus on the intelligence information swirling all around you, then you can reap the benefits of cognitive insights about the future.

When I managed money for a living, I wasn't a professional gambler. I didn't place big audacious bets with my client's hard-earned investment capital. Instead, I was prudent, cautious, and keenly aware at all times of the macro and micro indications of what the next day, month, or year might hold. It can be said that we make our own future, one decision at a time, and that's probably a true statement. The problem is we live our lives without understanding how our actions on any given day actually altered the trajectory of our lives.

The same holds true if you are a decision maker in an organization. Your actions have consequences. Of course, we viscerally understand when those decisions are monumental in scope. Signing closing documents to sell your business is an easy departure point from a known past and into an unknown future. Subtly grooming two or three executives over time to be your replacement doesn't have the same clarity. Which one will be the right one? Will one or more leave before it's time for you to decide? What if you choose an executive who thinks differently than you? Where will they lead the organization after you are gone? If you are a parent, deciding to take one job over another can have the same effect on the future.

Steering Small Changes

Spotting micro trends is tough but it's doable. As with most things in life, to become competent at this exercise you need to practice, fail, practice, and fail again. It takes years for poker players to learn the art of sizing up an adversary based only on visual cues. It will take you some time to master this method as well. The payoff can be huge. After four or five years managing money, I learned how to read my clients as well as the market. I paid attention, and it was worth the effort. I learned that everyone has a unique relationship with money. Some are emotional and others are passive aggressive. Some will tolerate minimum risk, while others will not. Here's the fascinating thing: they all cloak their true feelings and ask for the moon. What they told me wasn't reflective of how they really felt.

The markets also indicated small directional tendencies that indicated a possible change in momentum. The more I learned, the better I became at reading people and the markets as a prerequisite to making investment decisions. You may be in an industry, a market, or an economy that gives you vital clues every day, if only you pay attention. Steering small changes to align with micro trends is like diverting multiple streams of water toward a centerline. In time, the redirected flows join and become a river of momentum and change. Change you've anticipated and accelerated through direct involvement.

If you noticed that your daughter was late over and over again, what could you do to change the course of her personal history? If you noticed that a coworker or direct report was sliding off center at work, could you intervene and nudge them bit-by-bit back toward the right path? Micro trends provide us with leverage over the immediate future. Some build and build until they become macro trends. Study the initial stages of guerilla movements and you'll see what I mean. It was a cliché in the 1960s that a small ragtag group of ill-equipped rebels were sure to become an army that eventually overthrew the government. Small trends can become big trends. Pay attention to the tells!

Preparing for the Future

Preppers are people who store away food, batteries, just about everything needed to sustain life after a natural or manmade disaster. Some go as far as digging bunkers underground or, in extreme cases, purchasing old Cold War missile silos converted into vertical living habitats. People during the post-Great Depression years did the same thing. One group was anticipating worst-case scenarios, and the other learned they were not prepared when all the banks failed, and the world was plunged into chaos. When can we learn from these examples?

One of President Abraham Lincoln's favorite passages in the Bible has been paraphrased as, "This too shall pass." If you consider the trials that president endured, then you can see why he thought the phrase was universal in application. Both good and bad conditions and outcomes are fleeting when compared to the march of time. One constructive aspect of future thinking is that doing so places you in a stronger position when the winds of fate begin to blow. You will have the ability to anticipate and prepare for multiple scenarios when others, their heads stuck firmly in the proverbial sand of life, do not.

Anticipating outcomes in detail is an art. You won't always be right, but I'd venture to say you'll be as dialed in to the possibilities as anyone can be. A curious aspect of this intellectual exercise is the reputation you'll gain of saying what will likely happen before it does. It isn't due to voodoo magic; it's daily practice and discipline in the art of, "What if?" Navy SEALs and entrepreneurs need to be able to prepare thoughtfully for one or more potential outcomes. SEALs are often on their own in harm's way, or worse, on the run and looking for a way out. Entrepreneurs live on the edge of failure and success every day. A little understanding about the way forward is certainly a plus.

How should you prepare for the future? One way is education. What do you know about AI? What do you know about crypto currency? Autonomous land and air travel? Electric vehicles? Knowing about a thing is halfway to understanding the thing. I'm not saying you must agree, believe, or embrace that which you study; I only ask that you study. Engage in the mind race by matching your vision of the future with a continuous effort to understand trends large and small. The more in tune you are with the world around you, the easier it will be to feel "intuitive."

Another way to prepare is to go beyond a thought exercise to plotting out various paths and their effects. It's something military planners do all the time. Consequence analysis on an option-by-option basis. If this happens, then what? How about right after that? What will be affected, modified, radically changed, or destroyed by the selected future track, if it comes to pass? Then ask yourself, "Am I prepared for this particular outcome?" "What about my team, my company, my family?" If the answer is no, then you know what you must do. Mitigate the consequences.

In the special operations community, we like to say, "It is what it is." This may sound fatalistic, but it really means the future is now. Reality is now. It means suck it up and figure it out. Small, elite military units and business leaders don't have the luxury of holding endless meetings to look for answers. Time wasted is the difference between life or death, wealth or bankruptcy. Live and act in the now, but envision and prepare for the future, or multiple futures. Operating this way will make you different from all those around you, happy to lean on the past in ignorance, always surprised by what happens tomorrow. Be different. Thinking forward is the edge you need to survive and thrive in an ever-changing universe.

Chapter Nineteen

Be Different

In order to be irreplaceable one must always be different.
Coco Chanel

It's been a journey. From understanding the barriers to free and innovative thought, to learning how to envision and plan for the future. From the role and value of divergent thinking, to the value of convergent thinking and how that approach locks in your creative gains. I've been careful to note that in my rant against rules and obedience I refer almost without exception to the use of your mind. You were born with a gift; our species has evolved into sentient, creative beings who had to move, change, and adapt, or perish for hundreds of thousands of years. Navy SEALs and successful entrepreneurs must follow the laws of the land as well as the laws of nature. Bending or breaking rules is the way we test the static present in order to make room for a more colorful and satisfying future. If you're not convinced yet, I understand.

This philosophy may not be for everybody, but I do know that the successful leaders in every part of our shared world are transformative forces of positive energy. People who have learned to ignore the handcuffs and the red tape. People who see things the way they *might be* and race to that exciting point on the horizon. I like these types of people and try to emulate their powerful remedy for the past by studying and practicing their methods. I'm still a work in progress. Maybe I'll never measure up; but I'm convinced that this is a good thing, a noble pursuit, and I'll keep swinging until the good lord calls me.

Do you still have doubts? Being compliant is how we were all raised. Every school we attended, for some of us the military, and all the companies we've worked for prize an obedient student, service member, or employee. It's not for malicious reasons; instead, it's applied across the structure of society to keep us safe, in control. Free will isn't free if we blindly obey restrictions on the way we think. Freedom of expression isn't really free if we must guard our words and hide our ideas. I wrote this book after being a part of a wonderful organization focused for 30 years on under resourced kids.

As a board member of BEST Robotics, Inc., I was humbled by the amount of time professionals associated with the organization. Their time is dedicated to creating difficult technological challenges and mentoring teams of up to 20 students preparing for the annual competitive events. I watched as they cheered, eyes wet with tears of pride, watching teams of focused students as they executed their plans, collaborating and communicating, always with a smile on their faces.

My takeaways after the first year of my involvement were not intuitive. First, the mentors don't train or teach the teams of students. The students work through the difficulties themselves. They create a company, a website, a marketing plan and presentation, a commercial display booth, all while simultaneously designing and testing the robot they think will win. Second, the theme of the organization was all about Science, Technology, Engineering, and Math, or STEM learning. While the overall exercise did feature elements of STEM, it was so much more than that. Communications, marketing, website content development, and value proposition development are decidedly not STEM.

My third observation was that the students underwent an emotional and intellectual transformation as they progressed through the project. Rapid prototyping solutions, zooming in to handle the many details of the competition, and then back out again to put it all in the context of the deliverables. Finally, when actually watching a competition firsthand, I saw incredible teamwork, not just within each team but *between competing groups!* The participants bring boxes of cardboard, balsa wood, wires, small motors, batteries, and tools, lots of tools to the event. This is because they are allowed to observe and acknowledge performance failure in each competitive round. And then, in between rounds, they are encouraged to repair or redesign their robotic solution in preparation for the next engagement.

In one series of competitive rounds, a team realized it didn't have a specific item critical to their rapid prototyping effort. A student from another team overheard this and came over to help. Once he was made aware of the material item in question, he began to run from team to team, canvassing at least ten different groups before he found one with the item needed. Meanwhile, members of the other teams flowed over to see if they could assist. I watched dumbstruck as the special item was brought back to the table and a mixed crew from several teams lent a hand.

Competition is rarely a kumbaya thing. BEST Robotics fostered an intense desire to succeed without the all-too-human downside of envy, anger, and mistrust. The organization's executive director asked me to evaluate the entity from the perspective of an outsider stepping in. A person who was not an engineer, a technology expert, and frankly not fond of math. I accepted the challenge and began to ask questions, lots of questions. It was this experience that inspired me to write this book.

I began to see the purity of the students, untethered intellectually, untrained from a professional perspective, and unconcerned about climbing to the top over the backs of their teammates. Purity of thought without blind obedience to the frozen facts of science or the stodgy rules of mechanical engineering. I eventually found out that, while a handful of the participants did go on to engage in engineering or science, the majority did not, becoming successful and happy in all sorts of professions.

For 30 years BEST Robotics has been changing the world one child at a time. Providing an amazing experience in over 20 national events every year that are truly transformational. My study of this organization revealed the truth about ignorance. I'm reminded of a saying I saw once on a poster, "Remember, amateurs built the ark, professionals built the Titanic." When I say ignorance, I refer to a mind untainted by the heavy filters and restrictions of dogma expressed as rules. Pure thought requires ignorance to be set free. Free to discover, free to question.

So, I began my quest to understand. In time, I saw the beauty of the process, both individual, team, and between teams. An experiential transformative exercise in the art of possibility. What could adults and seasoned professionals learn from this example? I wasn't sure at first. Free or loose expression is an attribute normally associated with teenagers. I wondered if the human maturation process was to blame for our lost innocence. If so, it wasn't about impediments to creative thought, it was simply biology preparing us for adulthood. However, the more I investigated the BEST experience, the more I realized the classic conversion from dreamy-eyed teen to sober and stodgy adult was actually a regression of natural abilities, not the progression of maturity.

BEST MindLab

Soon, I began to study creativity in a more systematic fashion. Books, podcasts, webinars, and, of course, conversations with the incredible leaders of BEST Robotics. As I learned, I asked better questions. Many were easy to answer, a few not so much. In time it was clear that the BEST Robotics transformational experience crafted for the student participants was less about STEM-driven imperatives and more about intellectual adaptability and intense coordination. Every team operated like an enlightened think tank. Exploring *all* the possibilities rather than starting with hard truths and rules.

The Executive Director, Michael Steiner, had felt for some time that there was a secret sauce to it all, something that might be codified and extracted for use with adult professionals. Over time, a steady pace of academic debate, discussion, and introspective analysis convinced Michael, me, and the rest of the board of directors to transfer what we were discovering into a new delivery platform. This platform was focused on adult transformation or, as we found, more of a regression or default to our original brain functions related to innovation and creativity.

Starting with this premise, we developed a strategy and a battleplan to bring the secret sauce to corporations, academic institutions, and organizations of all sizes and shapes. My humble contribution was to turn it all into a for-profit entity. That entity was formed legally in mid-2023 and is called BEST MindLab, Inc. I focused initially on strategy. What was our collective vision? What was the purpose or point of the exercise? The answers were both straightforward business-driven conclusions and aspirational in nature.

We took our time, broadening our research. Michael, in particular, went out of his way to attend forward-thinking conferences on the state of innovation and creativity in society, business, and in all human endeavors. He also reached out to globally-recognized thought leaders in the area of human inspiration, creative energy, innovation, and that rarest of outcomes—invention. I was privileged to attend several of these individual sessions. People in Europe, the Middle East, Canada, and even Bali, all with exciting theories and a demonstrated path of proven application of their philosophies.

One national treasure discovered during Michael's quest for knowledge was a professor, Mark Runco. Mark had been leading university innovation centers and writing textbooks on creativity for decades. He lives and breathes the subject. After several meetings and reading many of his articles, Michael and I became diehard fans of his unique perspectives, intellect, and insight. My journey over an 18-month period was a surprise to me. Remember, I'm not an engineer, technology guru, or a professor of creativity. I couldn't build a robot if my life depended on it. What surprised me was how, in my case, intellectual humility and curiosity worked in concert to change the way I thought about creativity.

Somewhere along this learning curve I began to shape this book. I needed to show my work, to provide a rational, concise explanation on why we restrict our thoughts and dreams. I needed to understand why, as we age, we listlessly buy into the rules imposed on us and shutter our minds to the endless possibilities of life. The practical development of BEST MindLab also served as an additional catalyst for my personal epiphany.

It is one thing to observe and witness something as profound as the explosion of creativity displayed by the BEST Robotics' students and quite another to figure out how to apply that youthful spark to generations of older people, who are firmly convinced they are incapable of innovative thinking. It was this dual set of objectives, writing this book and forging BEST MindLab, that brought me the insights noted throughout *Be Different*.

Navy SEALs and Entrepreneurs

My subtitles act as a foreshadowing of the themes I wish to convey in my business books. As a former SEAL and current entrepreneur, I see a natural tendency for both groups to be nimble, to be visionary, and, yes, to be different regarding the use of their mental capabilities. People have studied success for as long as they have exercised cognitive awareness of their ability to emulate behavior.

The modern era of how-to books began with Napoleon Hill's book *Think and Grow Rich*. Published in the early twentieth century, this book sought to capture the magic of several successful people, personally interviewed by Hill to learn their secrets. Hill concluded that these documented characteristics of success were simple enough for anybody to follow. This is the essential promise of every how-to book today: we can learn and emulate and become transformed.

SEALs have existed in the United States Navy in one form or another since the beginning of World War Two, over 80 years ago as of this writing. The celebrated unit has stumbled, learned, excelled, and stumbled again. I am firmly convinced, from my personal involvement for 20 years and as a fan of history, that the root cause of this cyclical stumbling behavior is a rejection of the freewheeling and spirited exercise of creativity in exchange for the strict rules and guidelines associated with the Army and the Marines.

Since the beginning, maritime special units were valuable for their ability to do what larger, more conventional units could not do. Through World War Two, Korea, Vietnam, Grenada, Panama, the Gulf War, Operation Enduring Freedom in Afghanistan, and Operation Iraqi Freedom, our Navy's elite warriors have evolved and then devolved. Grown large and then shrunk almost to extinction. In the 1990s, the Naval Special Warfare Center in Coronado, California, initiated a series of recorded interviews covering the entire lifespan of modern naval special operations. The results were startling.

The interviews drew in men from every war. The questions sought to find both common ground and differences in how each generation of frogmen operated. The first and easiest conclusion based on these interviews was related to technology. Everything from radios, weapons, optics, navigation, and many more categories was, as you might expect, different. Most agreed that in principle a better tool was a good thing. However, almost to a man, they all believed a maritime warrior should not be turned into a pack mule simply because the technology existed. Lean and mean was the theme. At the time this was not the philosophy in the SEAL Teams. We were loading men down with upwards of 30 pounds more than our Vietnam veterans carried. This was a direct influence of the Army concept of each infantryman being able to carry everything required for a long duration engagement on their backs.

The second major takeaway was even more interesting. Remember, we were interviewing combat-experienced veterans across multiple decades and wars. Again, in near universal agreement, they said complexity in planning is a waste of time, and worse, it leads to failure on target more often than not. They usually added that the best plans were the ones that relied on reality and not blind application of prior plans or planning. A customized, case-by-case approach.

This observation again flew in the face of the trends at the time. I knew too well what they were saying. When I became a SEAL, we used the planning process developed in Vietnam. Keep it simple. Simple enough that everyone from the officer down to the newest guy on the team fully understood the intent. Think through the issues related to terrain, enemy capabilities, our capabilities, and the task or mission. Use your head and be prepared to improvise when reality shifts under your feet.

Keeping it simple wasn't all Vietnam-era SEALs did. The Vietnam War was the test bed for how SEALs operated and, yes, planned those extraordinarily successful operations. What I was told by these veterans had been proven in combat. It wasn't theoretical or designed to impress a room full of senior staff officers. It all relied on a foundation of intense individual and unit training in every aspect of our work. Standard operating procedures, or SOPs, that filled in all the planning gaps and then some. We were prepared *and* adaptable.

Then in the early 1980s, we began to grow, expanding to participate in major joint service and allied training exercises. We became self-conscious about our simplistic planning methods. Before long we began to adopt the Army Special Forces planning methods. Within a few years, our intuitive and professional, war-tested, SEAL-vetted processes were tossed aside in favor of three-hour-long dog and pony shows. Graphs and charts and endless discussion, the approved Army way. I can tell you from personal experience during this transition that creative solutions rarely survived the committee of officers listening to and scrutinizing every little detail of our operation. Our methods became homogenized. What made us special was diluted.

Entrepreneurs have been around since the first hominid traded a sharpened stone tool for food. We can all run off the names of famous entrepreneurs who've leveraged their innovative minds to change our world forever: Steve Jobs, Bill Gates, Elon Musk, Thomas Edison, Nikola Tesla, the list goes on and on. However, successful entrepreneurs are all around us, perhaps less famous, but no less innovative and impactful in their own way. I have had personal entrepreneurial success as well as failure. I've come to understand the two outcomes that come with the territory. Risk taking isn't always heads you win.

Maybe it's my SEAL background, but I never rest on my successes. I, instead, continually run the bad outcomes through my mind, analyzing every step on the way to failure. Winning is nice, but we learn from failing. It's how we all transitioned from crawling to walking and walking to running. Failures are packed with little packets of gold, lessons learned, large and small. Was it timing? Talent? Did I miss the obvious or did I ignore the obvious? Was I resourced appropriately? Was the goal even valid? I do this every day and try to become better.

Agility and flexibility are hallmarks of successful entrepreneurs. So is courage, conviction, and relentless execution. While not all ideas work out, entrepreneurs keep the ideas coming. They know instinctively that ideas are the result of experience and thinking differently about the past and the future. They evolve, grow, risk it all, and do so knowing the consequences of failure. It's when they begin to ignore their intelligence, their business muse, that they start to become conventional, safe. This shift in mindset is also an evolutionary process. Safety and stability. Maintain the status quo. Slow it all down; dumb it down, too.

Of course, you know by now that this state is not consistent with the reality of life and business. The atoms are constantly quivering, the universe is changing, and so are your competitors and customers. Just look at the life cycle of musical groups and musical genres. You must evolve and adapt or die. Slowly or incrementally, it makes little difference, the outcome is the same. Like the Navy SEAL experience, losing your creative way has consequences, and wrapping everything in layers of rules or avoiding risk isn't a recipe for sustained success.

Don't fall into the success trap. Live and act in the now, but envision and prepare for the future, or multiple futures. Keep your head on a swivel, anticipating change rather than becoming a victim of it. Operating in this manner will *make you different* from all those around you, who are happy to rely on the past in ignorant bliss, expecting the same thing every day and always startled when the world bangs a hard right.

If you need to bend the rules, do so. If you need to break rules to push past apathy, go for it! If you need to pave your own road, make your own new set of rules based on the future, be my guest! Thinking forward is the edge you need to survive and thrive in our ever-changing universe. Being creative as a child will lead to innovation and invention. Trust me, you're never too old to think again. *Be different!*

About the Author

Marty Strong is the author of *Be Nimble: How the Creative Navy SEAL Mindset Wins on the Battlefield and in Business*, the first in a series of business leadership books revealing his unique perspective and insight. *Be Visionary: Strategic Leadership in the Age of Optimization*, Marty's second book, reflects his personal and professional journey crafting and applying strategic thinking as a Navy SEAL officer and as a corporate CEO. After his 20-year military service, Marty became a successful high-net-worth investment advisor with the Union Bank of Switzerland. Marty moved on from UBS after seven years to become a successful senior vice president for a billion-dollar-a-year defense contracting company. Since 2009, Marty has led several businesses as CEO and Chief Strategy Officer. Marty serves both on profit and nonprofit boards, and is a sought-after motivational speaker.

Note to Readers

Thank you for investing your precious time and hard-earned money on *Be Different*. I admire people who seek new insights, and by finishing this book you have truly embraced the possibilities the future holds. If you have a few moments, please feel free to add your review of my book to your favorite online site. Feedback is always welcome. Please visit my author, consulting, and speaking website, www.martystrongbenimble.com, for news on upcoming works or to read my most recent blog posts.

Sincerely,
Marty Strong

BUSINESS
BOOKS

Business Books

Business Books publishes practical guides
and insightful non-fiction for beginners and professionals.
Covering aspects from management skills, leadership and
organizational change to positive work environments, career
coaching and self-care for managers, our books are a valuable
addition to those working in the world of business.

15 Ways to Own Your Future
Take Control of Your Destiny in Business
and in Life
Michael Khouri
A 15-point blueprint for creating better collaboration,
enjoyment, and success in business and in life.

Paperback: 978-1-78535-300-0 ebook: 978-1-78535-301-7

The Common Excuses of the Comfortable Compromiser
Understanding Why People Oppose
Your Great Idea
Matt Crossman
Comfortable compromisers block the way of anyone trying to
change anything. This is your guide to their common excuses.

Paperback: 978-1-78099-595-3 ebook: 978-1-78099-596-0

The Failing Logic of Money
Duane Mullin
Money is wasteful and cruel, causes war, crime and
dysfunctional feudalism. Humankind needs happiness, peace
and abundance. So banish money and use technology and
knowledge to rid the world of war, crime and poverty.

Paperback: 978-1-84694-259-4 ebook: 978-1-84694-888-6

Mastering the Mommy Track
Juggling Career and Kids in Uncertain Times
Erin Flynn Jay
Mastering the Mommy Track tells the stories of everyday
working mothers, the challenges they
have faced, and lessons learned.

Paperback: 978-1-78099-123-8 ebook: 978-1-78099-124-5

Modern Day Selling
Unlocking Your Hidden Potential
Brian Barfield
Learn how to reconnect sales associates with customers
and unlock hidden sales potential.
Paperback: 978-1-78099-457-4 ebook: 978-1-78099-458-1

The Most Creative, Escape the Ordinary,
Excel at Public Speaking Book Ever
All the Help You Will Ever Need in Giving
a Speech
Philip Theibert
The 'everything you need to give an outstanding speech'
book, complete with original material
written by a professional speechwriter.
Paperback: 978-1-78099-672-1 ebook: 978-1-78099-673-8

On Business And For Pleasure
A Self-Study Workbook for Advanced Business English
Michael Berman
This workbook includes enjoyable challenges and has been
designed to help students with the English they need for work.
Paperback: 978-1-84694-304-1

Small Change, Big Deal
Money as if People Mattered
Jennifer Kavanagh
Money is about relationships: between individuals and
between communities. Small is still beautiful, as peer
lending model, microcredit, shows.

Readers of ebooks can buy or view any of these bestsellers
by clicking on the live link in the title. Most titles are
published
in paperback and as an ebook. Paperbacks are available in
traditional bookshops. Both print and ebook formats
are available online.
Find more titles and sign up to our readers' newsletter at:
collectiveinkbusiness-books.com/
Facebook: facebook.com/CINonFiction/
Twitter: @CINonFiction